THIS BOOK IS DUE FOR RETURN BY :—

		15 NOV 1993
24 NOV 1978	26 OCT 1987	17 NOV 1993
17 NOV 1979	1 FEB 1987	15 NOV 1995
15 DEC 1979		
20 MAR 1980	29 NOV 1990 UCC LIBRARY	
	30 OCT 1991	22 MAR 1999
30 OCT 1980		CANCELLED
		UCC LIBRARY
3 APR 1981	27 NOV 1991	16 MAY 1999
28 NOV 1981		
		UCC LIBRARY
		23 MAY 1999 UCC LIBRARY
2 JUN 1986	17 DEC 1992	20 APR 2001
		UCC LIBRARY
		5 JUN 2002

THE BALLADS AND SONGS OF W. B. YEATS

THE BALLADS AND SONGS OF W. B. YEATS

The Anglo-Irish Heritage in Subject and Style

COLIN MEIR

Macmillan

First published 1974 by
THE MACMILLAN PRESS LTD
London and Basingstoke
Associated companies in New York
Dublin Melbourne Johannesburg and Madras

SBN 333 15839 3

Typeset in Great Britain by
COLD COMPOSITION LTD
Tunbridge Wells, Kent
and printed in Great Britain by
LEWIS REPRINTS LTD
London and Tonbridge

455845

Contents

Preface

Yeats is unavoidably a poet of two cultures, English and Anglo-Irish. Because his native language is English his artistic development owes much to English literary traditions, a matter which has been variously, if not perhaps exhaustively, dealt with by many hands. The Anglo-Irish heritage has, however, received comparatively little critical attention. Yet that heritage was important to Yeats, as is clearly shown in his published prose and his early journalism. Although he may at times be found saying one thing about Irish literature and doing something quite different in his own poetry, what he saw as distinctively Irish had a direct bearing on his theory and practice between 1886 and 1900; and what his later poetry owes to his native tradition has its beginnings in those early years when Yeats's critical energies so exclusively served deliberate Irish aims. This book first examines the effect on Yeats's work of his turning in the mid 1890s from the ideal of a popular national poetry to that of an esoteric literature which would perform a quasi-religious function for its people. The most important change in Yeats's development came after 1900. It was not until he had abandoned these ideals about the poet's role in Ireland that he was able to draw on the translations from the Gaelic which he now recognised as the central line of his native poetic tradition. The rest of the book deals mainly with what Yeats learned from this tradition, and with the influence — increasingly pervasive from 1904 onwards — of the syntax of Anglo-Irish dialect on his verse. Yeats's lifelong concern with the problems of subject, language and form testifies to his vitality as a poet; and it is nowhere more evident than in his ballads and songs. They illustrate the changes in Yeats's view of popular poetry and its audience, and mark predominant features in the evolution of his style.

In addition to those listed in the footnotes and bibliography, I wish to acknowledge my general debt to the following critical works which contain material relevant to my subject: E.A. Boyd, *Ireland's Literary Renaissance* (1916); Stephen Gwynn (ed.), *Scattering Branches* (1940); Louis MacNeice, *The Poetry of W.B.Yeats* (1941); Robin Flower, *The Irish Tradition* (1947); T.R.Henn, *The Lonely Tower* (1950); Robin Skelton and Anne Saddlemyer (eds), *The World of W.B.Yeats* (1965); Daniel Hoffmann, *Barbarous Knowledge* (1967); Phillip Marcus, *Yeats and the Beginning of the Irish Renaissance* (1970).

I particularly wish to thank Donald Davie and George Dekker, both formerly at Essex University, for their guidance and encouragement in this study in its initial form. I also wish to thank the following persons for advice and/or bibliographical information: F.J.Byrne, University College, Dublin; Jacques Chuto, University of Paris; D.W.Cole, McGill University; J.H.Delargy, Irish Folk Lore Commission; Oliver Edwards; G.S.Fraser, Leicester University; T.R.Henn, Cambridge University; P.L.Henry, University College, Galway; A.N.Jeffares, Stirling University; Roger McHugh, University College, Dublin; Thomas Parkinson; Peter Strevens, Essex University; Thomas Ward, Irish Folk Lore Commission; Michael B.Yeats.

Permission to reprint extracts from the following works was given by the Macmillan Publishing Co. Inc., New York: *The Collected Poems of W. B. Yeats*, 'Adam's Curse', copyright 1903 by Macmillan Publishing Co. Inc., renewed 1931 by William Butler Yeats; 'Down by the Salley Gardens', 'The Lamentation of the Old Pensioner', 'The Valley of the Black Pig', 'A Poet to His Beloved', 'The Ballad of Moll Magee', 'The Ballad of Father Gilligan', 'The

I Popular Nationalism 1885-1892

The most important event in Yeats's early life was his meeting in 1885 with John O'Leary, the old Fenian leader who had recently returned to Ireland from political exile. O'Leary gave a direction to the young poet's ambition by introducing him to nineteenth century Anglo-Irish literature and inspiring him to feel he had a vital role to play in its development. Yeats attended meetings of the 'Young Ireland' Society, of which O'Leary was President, where literary readings were given and Irish matters passionately debated. Years later he declared: 'From these debates,from O'Leary's conversation, and from the Irish books he lent or gave me has come all that I have set my hand to since.'[1]

Most of the poetry Yeats read under O'Leary's guidance was published in countless ballad books which had an enormous circulation, one of the best known being Charles Gavan Duffy's *Ballad Poetry of Ireland* (1845). In the main this popular poetry came from two separate Irish traditions: that of the patriotic verse written by numerous literate nineteenth century Irishmen, few of whom had any real talent; and that of a relatively small number of translations from the Gaelic which came out of a rich and long-established poetic tradition, oral and written, folk and literary. Apart from the translations there was little enough for Yeats to work on; indeed one of the most remarkable things about Yeats's achievement is that he became a major poet whose verse is distinctively Anglo-Irish out of a native background which, in comparison with the mainstream of English literature, was on the whole paltry in quality. But what is important to Yeats's beginnings is that he had inherited a popular tradition, unequal as it was; that, moreover, he believed he had an audience he could educate. In his own work his first move was to find the right subjects and the right language; in his criticism he extolled the virtues of a ballad literature.

Yeats soon discovered that two Irish poets stood out from all the rest. Mangan and Ferguson had both written a substantial body of work which was only selectively represented in the ballad books. Yeats linked his name with theirs and with that of Davis in these frequently quoted lines from 'To Ireland in the Coming Times':

> Nor may I less be counted one
> With Davis, Mangan, Ferguson.

But when he claimed in 1892 that the three writers shared a 'community in the treatment of Irish subjects after an Irish fashion'[2], he was over-simplifying the truth about their poetry and what he saw in it.

Thomas Davis (1815-45) was the highly esteemed leader of the Young Ireland political movement of the 1840s. His verse and that of his followers appeared in *The Nation* newspaper, the organ of the movement, between 1842 and 1845 and was published under the title *The Spirit of the Nation*, a volume which was in its fiftieth edition by 1870. Although he did write one or two songs which, because they were based on folk sources, avoided the political bombast typical of that volume, and one lament which Yeats consistently praised, Davis's characteristic style was frequently as flatly derivative as the following:

> When boyhood's fire was in my blood
>   I read of ancient freemen,
> For Greece and Rome who bravely stood,
>   Three hundred men and three men.
> And then I prayed I yet might see
>   Our fetters rent in twain,
> And Ireland, long a province, be
>   A NATION ONCE AGAIN.
>
>   ('A Nation Once Again')

Davis's subject matter was Irish in that he emphasised heroic rebellion and proclaimed the need for unity and freedom, but his form was taken from the English literary ballads of Scott and Macaulay. Yeats never deluded himself about the quality of this political verse, but he did praise Davis and it was on such work that Davis's popular fame rested.

The poetry of James Clarence Mangan (1803-49) was of a different kind. Although he produced some political doggerel for *The Nation,* his work as a whole has nothing to do with the Young Ireland tradition. Both his original verse and his translations, made from several languages including Gaelic, are deeply marked by his own personality; and Yeats soon recognised that his style at its best had an intensity which raised him above any of his contemporaries. His fame as a popular poet is based mainly upon 'Dark Rosaleen', a free translation of the Gaelic song 'Roisin Dubh', which deservedly became the most widely known nationalist poem of the century. Its energy and verve set it quite apart from the trite verse of *The Spirit of the Nation;* ostensibly a love song, it is not until the last stanza that the identification of Rosaleen with Ireland is confirmed:

> O! the Erne shall run red
>   With redundance of blood,
> The earth shall rock beneath our tread,
>   And flames wrap hill and wood,
> And gun-peal, and slogan cry,
>   Wake many a glen serene,
> Ere you shall fade, ere you shall die,
>   My Dark Rosaleen!
>   My own Rosaleen!
> The Judgement Hour must first be nigh,
> Ere you can fade, ere you can die,
>   My Dark Rosaleen!

Though simple in its reliance on repetitive effects, that is splendid rhetoric; and all the more so since it is Mangan's own. Mangan always speaks through his translations, but his sources help to modify the exaggerated fervour or self-pity which is sometimes heard in his personal verse. A prolific and extremely uneven writer, he is nevertheless the most talented nineteenth century Irish poet before Yeats, and not only in a simple popular strain, principally because of the quality of passion Yeats praised in him.

Sir Samuel Ferguson (1810-86) made several excellent translations of Gaelic songs which in rhythm and diction were to provide a source for Yeats's own poetry, both early and late; and it is for the most part in this work alone that he can be regarded as anything of a popular poet. But Ferguson's initial importance to Yeats also lay in the fact that he wrote epic poetry about Ireland's mythological heroes. It was very different from the work of either Davis or Mangan, as can be seen from the following lines quoted by Yeats from 'Conary' in his first article on the poet in 1886:[3]

> One I saw
> Seated apart; before his couch there hung
> A silver broidered curtain; grey he was,
> Of aspect mild, benevolent, composed.
> A cloak he wore, of colour like the haze
> Of a May morning, when the sun shines warm
> On dewy meads and fresh-ploughed village land.

Yeats argued that Ferguson wrote such poetry for the people of Ireland, though it was very clear that the people did not read it.

Yeats genuinely admired the work of Mangan and Ferguson, but he had his priorities right in listing Davis first in 'To Ireland in the Coming Times'. It was plain that Davis was pre-eminently the nation's popular poet and that his example had brought a proliferation of political verse into the many ballad books published since the 1840s. Yeats's excitement at reading these books came from the abundant evidence they gave that Ireland had a ready-made audience for poetry, an audience whose capacity for passion he admired even though he regarded much of the verse that elicited it as being at best an adulterated art. If John O'Leary, before whom Yeats said he stood as 'the poet before his theme',[4] could admit that he owed his patriotism to the poems of Thomas Davis while at the same time he did not claim much for them as literature, what then, Yeats felt, would a good tradition do for Ireland? Merely being a practising Irish poet, however, was not enough. In his letters, and particularly in his journalism, Yeats took up the case for a national literature and tried to define its nature and function. It was a process which involved a critical assessment of what was worthwhile in the Anglo-Irish heritage, but the resulting arguments about what that tradition had been and what it was to be suffered from the prejudice of Yeats's concern to capture Davis's audience: the term 'national poet' had an ambivalence which he could not at first resolve.

1 THE SUBJECTS OF IRISH POETRY

> The school of writers I belonged to tried to found itself on much of the subject matter of this poetry, and, what was almost more in our thoughts, to begin a more imaginative tradition in Irish literature, by a criticism at once remorseless and enthusiastic.[5]

Yeats's commentary here vaguely passes over in the phrase 'almost more in our thoughts' the fact that between 1888 and 1892 his critical theory was geared to the demands of literary nationalism in a way that he later declared had harmed his own development as a poet. Yeats's self-imposed role of public mentor of a renascent literature compromised his private view that poetry is the voice of personal feeling. Very early on he had determined:

> We should write out our thoughts in as nearly as possible the language we thought them in, as though in a

letter to an intimate friend. We should not disguise them in any way, for our lives give them force as the lives of people in plays give force to their words.[6]

Naive as its formulation was at this stage, this theory with its characteristic emphasis on the personality of the poet became the basis for Yeats's work after 1900. His concern, however, to 'unite literature to the passion for patriotism and ennoble both thereby'[7] for a time led him astray from his personal ideals on what the subjects and language of poetry should be.

In trying to set up criteria for a literature which would help to create a sense of nationality, Yeats stressed that a poet should write about Ireland, not merely about himself The poetry of William Allingham (1824-89) is perhaps best summed up in the title of one of his poems, 'Let me Sing of what I Know', but for Yeats in 1888 this was not enough. He commended Allingham's lyricism and the possession of a regional landscape evoked by his verse; he praised him as an artist, but said that his lack of sympathy with national life and history had limited his vision, 'driven away from his poetry much beauty and power . . . thinned his blood'.[8] With reference to one of Allingham's longer poems, 'The Music Master', Yeats commented:

> The personal nature of the sadness of this poem again divides Allingham from Davis and Ferguson. They were essentially national writers. Davis, looking into the future, saw Ireland free and prospering. Ferguson saw her in the past before the curse had fallen. For her were their hopes and memories. They ever celebrated the national life. No matter what they described you were made to feel its relation to that life. Allingham, though always Irish, is no way national.[9]

In the same way Yeats defined the limitations of his own novel, *John Sherman* (1891), which, although it described a 'typical Irish feeling', was not national; it had, he said, 'a

West of Ireland feeling . . . for, like that of Allingham for Ballyshannon, it is West rather than National.'[10] Yeats had chosen Ferguson as an example of a national poet because he claimed, with some validity, that Ferguson's epic poetry re-created the sense of Ireland's heroic past. But he knew that this work had not gained Ferguson a wide audience; on the other hand, the inclusion of Davis marks the extent to which, as public spokesman for his native literature, Yeats felt he must acknowledge the work of its most public poet. It was not, however, merely propoganda; for Yeats later said that Davis's political poetry had corrupted his instinctive love of place and had prevented him from giving a more profound picture of Ireland in his own verse:

> Allingham and Davis have two different kinds of love of Ireland. In Allingham I find the entire emotion for the place one grew up in which I felt as a child. Davis on the other hand was concerned with ideas of Ireland, with conscious patriotism. His idea of Ireland was artificial, an idea built up in a couple of generations by a few commonplace men. This artificial idea has done me as much harm as the other has helped me.[11]

That is Yeats in 1909. In the twenty years which separate these comments on Allingham and Davis two important changes occurred in Yeats's conception of the poet's role in Ireland, ending finally in a complete about-face. Whereas in 1888 to be personal and Irish does not meet Yeats's requirements for a national poet, in 1908 it is precisely in those terms that nationality in literature is described: 'It is the presence of a personal element alone that can give [art] nationality in a fine sense, the nationality of its maker.'[12] Again, whereas in 1888 Yeats had turned to memories of the past in Ferguson's epics and to hopes for the future in Davis's verse, in 1904 his emphasis is on the present and the personal:

> [National literature] is the work of writers who are moulded by influences that are moulding their country,

and who write out of so deep a life that they are
accepted there in the end. . . . I mean by deep life that
men should put into their writing the emotions and ex-
periences that have been most important to themselves.[13]

It was not until he had rediscovered this principle for himself by getting rid of specific national ideals that Yeats was
able to apply himself to that other aspect of his youthful
aim, the finding of a natural language. In the meantime,
however, his sense of what the language of Irish poetry
should be was to pass through two extremes; and in each
case the idea of language was integral with a particular
concept about Irish subject matter and a particular kind of
audience.

2 IRISH FORMS AND LANGUAGE

Right from the beginning Yeats saw the tradition of Anglo-
Irish poetry as developing out of the translations from the
Gaelic, but not until the mid 1890s did he properly distinguish them from the poetry of Young Ireland. In
'Popular Ballad Poetry of Ireland', an article contributed
to *Leisure Hour* in November 1889, Yeats stated that 'the
true ballad — the poem of the populace' had been driven
away in England. Popular ballad literature, he said, re-
quires that national traditions be alive in the minds of the
people, not hidden away in libraries; second, that 'the
poets and the populace shall have one heart — that there
shall be no literary class with its own way of seeing things
and its own conventions.' That such conditions prevailed
in the predominantly oral Gaelic culture explains, Yeats
argued, why Ireland has in recent times a tradition of
balladry upon which — first through translations and then
through original work — the new written literature in
English was being built. Ignoring the fact that the translations were frequently made from the work of poets who
were justifiably proud of their professionalism, Yeats defined them as 'a simple and spontaneous . . . peasant-poet

craft'. And because those translations did have a wide audience, Yeats saw them as evidence of a vigorous popular balladry whose line of tradition was continued by the Young Ireland movement. He was right in that both the translators and the Young Irelanders shared the same popular audience, but he was soon to think very differently about their respective national traditions; and when he claimed that the Irish ballad was a 'poem of the populace' he was arguing in quite untenable primitivistic terms.

The distinction between the literary and the balladic was ambiguously applied to the poetry of Ferguson. Although he later admitted that Ferguson was not a popular poet,[14] in his second article on him Yeats claimed that his verse appealed 'to the great concourse of the people . . . to the universal emotions', in contrast to 'almost all the poetry of this age written by students, for students'.[15] Similarly, Yeats marked the change of style in the work of a contemporary poet, John Todhunter, whose verse play *Helena in Troas* (1886) he stigmatised as 'essentially an art product . . . [it] essentially belongs to what is called poetical poetry, everything seen through the spectacles of books'; whereas Todhunter's 'Children of Lir' (1888), a narrative poem based on Irish legend, Yeats declared was 'ethnic', written in 'strangely unstudied, fluid and barbaric measures'.[16] Yeats then went on to contrast English literature which, because it was in its 'old age', had grown so indirect and complex that it was 'only a possession for the few', with Todhunter's poems which he asserted belonged 'to Ireland and to youth'.[17] Backed by familiar features of late nineteenth century primitivism, Yeats here carried his argument to the point of absurdity. While Ireland's literature in English remained undifferentiated in syntax and idiom from the work of English writers, it was nonsense to claim that the truly Irish poet was naturally free from the sophistication and elaboration which Yeats, rightly or wrongly, attributed to a literature in its 'old age'.

Up to 1892 Yeats's journalistic criticism was tediously

consistent in such assumptions about the distinctiveness of Irish style; indeed it is surprising how far he could go in propagandising for a literature which he insisted was both popular and national. Clearly he was at this time prepared to tolerate sentimentality in what a poem said for the sake of a simplicity in the saying which avoided the blatant political rhetoric of Young Ireland verse. Nevertheless, one important principle does emerge from this criticism. Reviewing *Shamrocks* (1887), the second volume of verse by Katharine Tynan, Yeats said her work had come much nearer to Goethe's ambition to write not of the metaphors of things but of the things themselves:

> This, in its most verbal sense, is true of the difference between Miss Tynan's first book and her second . . . in the second the things themselves are often painted with passionate and careful fidelity . . . not that the first method is not beautiful in its degree, but the second must ever be the main thing. This I say dogmatically, believing there are no two sides to the question.[18]

Writing of the things themselves is exactly the quality Yeats sought in his own work after 1900 when he had become tired of 'that artificial English so many of us played with in the nineties',[19] a quality which he found so vividly present in peasant speech that he practised translating his verse and prose into Anglo-Irish dialect in order to rid his style of vagueness and abstractions. But he had already found it, if only fortuitously, in some of the poems he wrote before 1892.

3 YEATS'S EARLY BALLADS

Yeats decided very early on that his own subject matter was to be Irish. In preparing his first volume for the press, he determined that if the number of poems was to be reduced, 'the Irish poems must be kept, making the personality of the book'.[20] That first volume, *The Wanderings of Oisin and Other Poems* (1889), did in fact contain a

number of poems which had nothing at all to do with
Ireland, but by 1895 Yeats had jettisoned most of them,
leaving the titles* almost exactly as they are now listed
under *Crossways* and *The Rose* in his *Collected Poems;* and
in 1899 he asserted that he had always written as an Irish
writer and with Ireland in his mind. But even the most
cursory reading of Yeats's early work confirms that Irish
subject matter did not consistently give rise to a distinctively Irish style. In particular, where Yeats consciously
attempted to meet the criteria he laid down for a national
literature in poems published up to 1891, the result was far
from wholly successful.

Following the principle that all good literature must be
popular, the four poems with the word 'ballad' in their
titles were written with a deliberate national aim. 'I
wished', Yeats said, 'to be as easily understood as the
Young Ireland writers, — to write always out of the
common thought of the people'. He explains that to
escape the rhetoric, the 'patriotic extravagance' of those
poets, he tried 'to write of nothing but emotion, and in the
simplest language'; and he points out that initially he chose
poems of Mangan and Davis as a standard of what could be
easily understood, but that in his efforts to imitate them
he became trivial and sentimental, though Mangan and
Davis at their best were never so.[21] Certainly, Yeats's early
ballads bear little resemblance to the work of either of
these poets, but his thinking of Davis as a model pertinently suggests the direction of his ambition. Yeats never
denied Davis's influence of men's actions; for all his reser-
vations about their literary achievement, he was able to
praise the Young Irelanders for having 'taught fervour and
labour and religious toleration'.[22] And it was partly perhaps because Yeats understood how simple that moral
idealism was that he made the thought so simple in his
own ballads. But it was also an aesthetic choice: in one of
his several apologies for the sentimentality of his early

*Wherever Yeats's revisions of a poem are only minor ones, the final
printing as in *Collected Poems* (1950) is given throughout this text.

verse, Yeats points out that he refused to permit it any share of an intellect which he considered impure.[23]

The four ballads are all based on prose accounts of various kinds.[24] Finding his subjects in this way, Yeats was practising what he preached. He edited his *Fairy and Folk Tales of the Irish Peasantry* (1888) with the intention that it should be used as a source book. As he told Katharine Tynan, he found the work laborious but worth doing 'for all the material for poetry, if nothing else. You and I will have to turn some of the stories into poems'.[25] That such a process was, however, somewhat mechanical is suggested by an earlier comment:

> Then I begin an Irish story; I do not believe in it, but it may do for some Irish newspaper and give me practice. .. [I] have been busy in the British Museum making up material for a story about Father John O'Hart.[26]

Yeats's ballads show that he was working on his material from the outside. Using a simple narrative line — as he does here more deliberately than in any other of his early poems — and aiming at the same time to evoke a simple emotion, he comes precariously close to what is merely puerile or banal; but the fault lies not so much in the simplicity of the story as in the nature of the emotion and the way it is evoked. 'The Ballad of Moll Magee', for example, is marred by religious sentimentalism and an appeal to sympathy, seen particularly in its last two stanzas:

> And sometimes I am sure she knows
> When, openin' wide His door,
> God lights the stars, His candles,
> And looks upon the poor.
>
> So now ye little childer,
> Ye won't fling stones at me;
> But gather with your shinin' looks
> And pity Moll Magee.

Only one stanza escapes the pity-begging tone of the poem:

> The windows and the doors were shut,
> One star shone faint and green,
> The little straws were turnin' round
> Across the bare boreen.

Here the predicament and the mood are effectively given in the details described.

'The Ballad of Father Gilligan' makes use of commentary and dialogue, and this variety in itself saves the poem from being as tedious as 'Moll Magee'. The story — of how God relieved the weary Father Gilligan of his duty in visiting a dying parishioner — is told with the simplicity and economy Yeats wanted to achieve, but it remains nothing more than an incident. Father Gilligan's prayer of thankfulness is stuck on at the end of the poem:

> He Who is wrapped in purple robes,
> With planets in His care,
> Had pity on the least of things
> Asleep upon a chair.

As in the penultimate stanza of 'Moll Magee', Yeats was here reaching for a 'national' dimension in his verse by appealing to the religious consciousness of the Irish. In 'The Ballad of the Foxhunter' the story he chose to write about has no national relevance at all, but it too is vitiated by a sentimental treatment. In the first printing of the poem its last two stanzas read as follows:

> 'Now huntsman Rody, blow thy horn —'
> Die off the feeble sounds:
> And gazing on his visage worn,
> Are old and puppy hounds;
>
> The oldest hound with mournful din,
> Lifts slow his wintry head:
> The servants bear the body in —
> The hounds keen for the dead.

Again, what we get here is a constant appeal to feeling rather than the creation of it. Yeats has fallen into the same error Wordsworth sometimes made of loading insignificant objects with too much emotion, and the result is a banality verging on the comical, which even the later revisions do not entirely eradicate.

'The Ballad of Father O'Hart' is the only one of the four which steers clear of sentimentality, and that is because in this poem Yeats merely states what happened. It is also the only one whose theme is in any way political. Set in the Penal days in Ireland when Catholics were forbidden to own landed property, its opening lines describe how Father John was cheated by the Protestant to whom, in order to evade the law, he had given nominal possession of his estate:

> Good Father John O'Hart
> In Penal days rode out
> To a shoneen who had free lands
> And his own snipe and trout.
>
> In trust took he John's lands;
> Sleiveens were all his race;
> And he gave them as dowers to his daughters,
> And they married beyond their place.

But then, instead of making a nationalistic issue out of the situation — as many of his readers may have expected — Yeats turns the poem's meaning on an irony that is rather equivocal. Certainly, however, such a topic in the hands of the Young Irelanders would have been presented in rhetorical clichés of resentment and revenge.

Although Yeats's later comments on what he was trying to do can be somewhat contradictory,[27] it is clear that he felt his first sustained attempt to use Irish subject matter, in 'The Wanderings of Oisin', was too derivative in style. The syntax and the diction of the four ballads show a striking contrast to the language of the Oisin poem, but merely to tell a story in a simple manner is not to have found a distinctive Irish style. The Irishness of these poems lies only in proper names and place names, together with the occasional word not found in standard English usage.

4 YEATS'S 'IRISH' POEMS

Significantly enough, when Yeats spoke of what was 'Irish' in his early poetry he did not refer to the four ballads at all. The poems he names are: 'To an Isle in the Water', 'An Old Song Re-Sung' (the original title of 'Down by the Salley Gardens'), 'A Faery Song', 'The Lamentation of the Old Pensioner', 'The Lake Isle of Innisfree', and 'Love Song' (published in 1888 in *The Poems and Ballads of Young Ireland,* but never reprinted in any of Yeats's own volumes).[28] Yeats distinguished his 'Irish' poems from his more literary work, but in naming them and not the ballads he is tacitly defining an Irish poem as one that is not narrative but lyrical. In 'Moll Magee' and 'Father Gilligan', because the syntax is organised solely for the purpose of telling the story, and because the emotion is not part of the story but is stuck on to it from the outside — a contrivance betrayed in the sentimentality of these poems — there is no clear evocation of feeling. In the 'Irish' poems, on the other hand, the feeling is founded on the reality of the things named or the actions described (which are not the actions of narrative). 'The Lake Isle of Innisfree', for example, is sharply distinguishable in these terms from the early ballads:

> I will arise and go now, and go to Innisfree,
> And a small cabin build there, of clay and wattles made:
> Nine bean-rows will I have there, a hive for the
>   honey-bee,
> And live alone in the bee-loud glade.

The world Yeats wishes to escape to is particularised in things to have, to see and to hear; what he is escaping from is given in one line: 'While I stand on the roadway, or on

the pavements grey', which succinctly points the need for
the simple, solitary life the poem describes, and justifies
the biblical 'I will arise and go . . .' with its suggestion that
this act is nothing less than an act of truth to one's own
nature. Further glosses on the poem's meaning — such as
the colours in the second stanza contrasting with the
colourless street, or the fact that the linnet's wings suggest
joy, or that water suggests the healing of the spirit — are all
part of the concreteness of the evocation.

Yeats points to 'Innisfree' as an example of his beginning 'to loosen rhythm as an escape from rhetoric and
from that emotion of the crowd that rhetoric brings',[29] but
in referring to this poem as 'my first lyric with anything in
its rhythm of my own music' he failed to acknowledge
that its rhythm had been heard before in some of the
translations of Gaelic songs. Here is part of the opening
stanza of Ferguson's 'The Fair Hills of Ireland':

> There is honey in the trees where her misty vales
>   expand,
> And her forest paths in summer are by falling waters
>   fanned;
> There is dew at high noontide there, and springs i' the
>   yellow sand,
> On the fair hills of holy Ireland.

The rhythms and stresses of this translation are very close
to those in Yeats's poem; so also is the language usage: the
same simple verb forms, the same preponderance of things
named to evoke feeling.

Whereas 'Innisfree' is based on Yeats's personal experience, three of the other five poems he defined as 'Irish' are
taken wholly or in part from the lips of the people.
Indeed, it could be argued that the most famous of them is
an almost exact copy of a folk song:

'Down by the Sally Gardens' (Old country love song)

> Down by the Sally gardens my own true love and I did
>   meet .

She passed the Sally gardens, a tripping with her snow
    white feet.
She bid me take life easy just as the leaves fall from each
    tree;
But I being young and foolish with my true love would
    not agree.

In a field beside the river my lovely girl and I did stand,
And leaning on her shoulder I pressed her burning hand.
She bid me take life easy, just as the stream flows o'er
    the weirs
But I being young and foolish I parted her that day in
    tears.

I wish I was in Banagher and my fine girl upon my knee.
And I with money plenty to keep her in good company.
I'd call for liquor of the best with flowing bowls on
    every side.
Kind fortune ne'er shall daunt me, I am young and the
    world's wide.

In a note to the manuscript of this song in the National
Library, Dublin, P.J.McCall says that it was copied down
from memory and that he heard it sung about the year
1875.[30] Yeats's poem reads:

'Down by the Salley Gardens'

Down by the salley gardens my love and I did meet;
She passed the salley gardens with little snow-white feet.
She bid me take love easy, as the leaves grow on the
    tree;
But I, being young and foolish, with her would not agree.

In a field by the river my love and I did stand,
And on my leaning shoulder she laid her snow-white
    hand.
She bid me take life easy, as the grass grows on the
    weirs;
But I was young and foolish, and now am full of tears.

A footnote to its first publication in 1889 explains that 'this is an attempt to reconstruct an old song from three lines imperfectly remembered by an old peasant woman in the village of Ballysodare, Sligo, who often sings them to herself'; but Yeats had earlier told Katharine Tynan that his poem 'follows very closely the old ballad "Going to Mass last Sunday my True Love passed me by" '[31] – a confusion which may not be as deliberate as it sounds. If, despite its unproved dating, McCall's poem can be taken as the true source, we can see how Yeats smoothes out the metre and, by omitting the vigorous last stanza, creates a wistfulness which is more in keeping with the lyricism of the 1890s. Other less obvious sources have been quoted for Yeats's poem, but they all confirm that he was here writing in a folk song tradition. As in 'Innisfree', the language achieves concentration in simplicity through the specific and concrete. The poem does not appeal for emotional response in any way; it does not need to, because the feeling is in what is stated.

'The Lamentation of the Old Pensioner' shares, if perhaps with less successful effect, the same characteristics as 'Down by the Salley Gardens'. Again the words were taken down from a peasant, though they were not this time the words of a song. The first printing reads as follows:

> I had a chair at every hearth,
> When no one turned to see
> With 'Look at that old fellow there;
> And who may he be?'
> And therefore do I wander on,
> And the fret is on me.
>
> The roadside trees keep murmuring –
> Ah, wherefore murmur ye
> As in the old days long gone by,
> Green oak and poplar tree!
> The well-known faces all are gone,
> And the fret is on me.

Yeats re-wrote the poem for its publication in *Early Poems and Stories* (1925):

> Although I shelter from the rain
> Under a broken tree,
> My chair was nearest to the fire
> In every company
> That talked of love or politics,
> Ere Time transfigured me.
>
> Though lads are making pikes again
> For some conspiracy,
> And crazy rascals rage their fill
> At human tyranny,
> My contemplations are of Time
> That has transfigured me.
>
> There's not a woman turns her face
> Upon a broken tree,
> And yet the beauties that I loved
> Are in my memory;
> I spit into the face of Time
> That has transfigured me.

The re-written version is quite obviously a more complex and more powerful poem, of the style of the Crazy Jane sequence in *Words for Music Perhaps;* it is also more rhetorical. To claim it as a completely new lyric, however, is to ignore that both poems emphasise a state of feeling which is evoked by the spare naming of things and stating of circumstance. The only part of the first version that justifies the opprobious criticism that 'his lament is suffused with self-pity'[32] is in the opening lines of the second stanza. Here the contorted structure of 'Ah, wherefore murmur ye', together with the archaic word usage and the vagueness of 'murmur' and 'murmuring' declare the intrusion of a style more familiarly early Yeatsean, which contrasts sharply with the refrain 'And the fret is on me', whose syntax and idiom is genuinely Anglo-Irish. There

was in any case more in its original sources than actually
appeared in the first printing of the poem. In Yeats's early
story 'A Visionary' (*The Celtic Twilight*, 1893) the old
peasant not only tells the substance of the first stanza,
using the vivid but matter-of-fact image of the chair by the
fire, but also speaks of the thorn tree that is used metaphorically in the 1925 version. Furthermore, the peasant's
cry in the story: 'God possesses the heavens — God
possesses the heavens — but He covets the world'[33] has
something of the assertive defiance of the voice in the
poem's final printing. Such an outburst is excluded from
the first version because it was alien to the mood of world
weariness that Yeats superimposed on his material in 1890.

A similar process is seen in Yeats's 'Love Song', whose
source was an unrhymed translation from the Gaelic in
Edward Walsh's *Irish Popular Songs* (1847):

> My hope, my love, we will proceed
> Into the woods, scattering the dews
> Where we will behold the salmon, and
>   the ousel in its nest,
> The deer and the roebuck calling,
> The sweetest bird on the branches warbling,
> The cuckoo on the summit of the green hill;
> And death shall never approach us
> In the bosom of the fragrant wood.

Out of which, Yeats made the following:

> 'Love Song' from the Gaelic
>
> My love, we will go, we will go, I and you,
> And away in the woods we will scatter the dew;
> And the salmon behold, and the ousel too;
> My love, we will hear, I and you, we will hear,
> The calling afar of the doe and the deer,
> And the birds in the branches will cry for us clear,
> And the cuckoo unseen in his festival mood;
> And death, oh my fair one, will never come near
> In the bosom afar of the fragrant wood.

Yeats changes Walsh's translation into a lilting verse; but the repetition that achieves this lilt also subtly affects the mood, bringing an incantatory dreaminess into what was merely simple statement. Both this poem and the first printing of 'The Lamentation of the Old Pensioner' show Yeats seeing his Irish subject-matter through Pre-Raphaelite eyes, and describing it with that 'effeminate . . . strained lyricism'[34] he was later to castigate even in the work of his esteemed William Morris. The distortion is, however, only slight in each case. In 'Love Song' the dreamy mood does not seriously mar the simple catalogue of fish, bird and beast whose life in the woods represents to the lovers an escape from death; and later, in the opening stanza of 'Sailing to Byzantium', the vivid naming of a similar catalogue of 'fish, flesh, or fowl' suffices to evoke a purely sensual existence whose condition the ageing poet now so acutely sees as that of 'dying generations'.

Neither 'To an Isle in the Water' nor 'A Faery Song' owes anything in language to Irish folk tradition, oral or written; but the former, like 'Innisfree' and 'Down by the Salley Gardens', carries its feeling by a combination of repetitive phrasing and the description of actions that are not strictly narrative. 'A Faery Song', on the other hand, is the only one of the poems listed whose mood is not given concrete identification. Although he declared that this poem was 'extremely Irish', Yeats here produced a lyricism that better fitted his own 'Celtic Twilight' emphasis on vague yearnings for the other-worldly than the true native tradition. In the poems which are from the folk, the nineties plangency that Yeats adds to his material does not obscure the vivid directness of the original.

Two other poems more properly belong to the group under discussion. Yeats acknowledged that the last two lines of 'A Cradle Song' were suggested by the words of a Gaelic song quoted in Gerald Griffin's *The Collegians* (1829); and that 'The Meditation of the Old Fisherman' was 'founded upon some things a fisherman said to me when out fishing in Sligo Bay'.[35] The theme of the latter poem is the contrast between the present and the past; in its first printing the last two stanzas read:

> The lines are not heavy, nor heavy the long nets
>   brown —
> Ah woe! full many a creak gave the creel in the cart
> That carried the fish for the sale in the far away
>   town,
> *When I was a boy with never a crack in my heart.*
>
> Proud maiden, ye are not so fair, when *his* oar
> Is heard on the water, as *they* were, the proud and
>   apart,
> Who paced in the eve by the nets on the pebbly
>   shore,
> *When I was a boy with never a crack in my heart.*

Although Yeats's diction and versification cloud them somewhat, the realistic observations of the fisherman can be seen in the statements about the heavy lines and nets, and the creak of the creel in the cart, to describe the big catches he used to make; the sound of the oar on the water that tells a woman her lover is returning; and, above all, the refrain, which did not undergo any of the revisions Yeats made to the rest of the poem in 1895. These lines have the same characteristics as Yeats's direct borrowings and, like them, are as clearly differentiated from the predominant style of his poetry between 1892 and 1900 as they are from the sentimentalism of the early ballads.

Yeats said of 'Love Song', adapted from Walsh's translation, that he knew 'nothing more impossibly romantic and Celtic';[36] and the kind of modifications he made to his sources shows that his criteria for the Irishness of this group of poems had more to do with mood than with manner. But his instinct about them was truer than he realised, for they carry an unmistakable Irish signature in their reliance on an unadorned substantival strength which, together with a syntax of straightforward statement, focusses with effective economy directly on the feeling that is being evoked. In his later ballads and songs Yeats uses a more vigorous common idiom, and his syntax becomes more mobile and flexible, carries more transitive drive; but the starkness and clarity of that mature style have their beginnings in this mere handful of early 'Irish' poems. Two of them, 'Innisfree' and 'Down by the Salley Gardens', quickly became, and have since remained, the most widely known of all his work, the latter being sometimes accorded the final honour of 'author anonymous'. Yeats never again so completely achieved his early ambition to be as popular as Thomas Davis and the Young Irelanders while writing on a different subject and in a different style.

II Imaginative Nationalism

Yeats continued to praise Irish literature in primitivistic terms up to 1893, but by this time a new note is being heard. In a review of Katharine Tynan's *Ballads and Lyrics* (1891) Yeats speaks of the virtue of Irish ballads and songs which were made 'from some passionate impulse of the moment', but asserts that the discipline of art is much needed in modern Irish writing:

> We can produce neither the merits nor the defects of that poetry in which all was done from sudden emotion, nothing from deliberate art.... Such periods cannot last. If literatures are to go on they must add art to impulse and temper their fire with knowledge.[1]

That same year, 1892, a qualification in similar terms is made about the work of another contemporary poet, Ellen O'Leary:

> Its very simplicity and sincerity have made it, like much Irish verse, unequal, for when the inspiration fails, the writer has no art to fall back upon. Nor does it show anything of studied adjective or subtle observations.[2]

Yeats's address in 1893 to the National Literary Society in Dublin, entitled 'Nationality and Literature',[3] shows how ambivalent his position had become. Yeats maintained that every literature must pass through three periods: the epic or ballad period, the dramatic, and the lyric — a progress characterised by a movement from 'unity to multiplicity, from simplicity to complexity'. Whereas English literature was now in its lyric stage, marked by concern with subtlety of emotion or mood, Irish literature, 'alone among the literatures of Europe', was still in its ballad or epic age, 'simple and primitive'. Poetry of a lyric age, Yeats argued, was characterised by three things: because it dealt with the subtle expression of subjective feelings, it became a 'mysterious cult . . . an almost secret religion made by the few for the few'; because such feelings were 'too impalpable to find any clear expression in action or in speech leading to action', lyric poetry required an elaborate complexity of language; and, thirdly, because 'the great passions know nothing of boundaries', lyric poetry was cosmopolitan. By contrast, Ireland's poetry, 'at the outset of a literary epoch', was 'still a poetry of the people in the main, for it still deals with the tales and thoughts of the people'; its language dealt simply and directly with its subject; and that subject was national 'because people understand character and incident best when embodied in life they understand and set amid scenery they know of'. Yeats concluded by appealing to Irish writers to devote themselves wholly to the making of literature, to understand that art demands labour, and to study great models in other literatures, not in order to imitate them but to learn from them the secret of style.

Yeats wanted the best of both worlds. He praised Irish literature as a poetry of the people, a statement which was in any case far from exact, and yet exhorted its writers to study their style in models from foreign literatures which he had been at pains to explain were at a totally different stage from that of Ireland, a stage which he had defined in terms of style as well as subject, and which he had emphasised it was vain for any literature to emulate or strive for before its due time. He argued that the virtue of Irish literature was that it was simple and primitive, yet he also wanted it to be consciously artistic. Nevertheless, despite its self-contradictions, it was a clever and persuasive piece of rhetoric, clearly geared to the cause of literary nationalism.

But Yeats was not as confident as he sounded. He was beginning to be disturbed about the idea of Ireland that lay behind his protestations about the distinctive virtues of its literature. Looking back on this period in 1908, he commented:

> We sought to make a more subtle rhythm, a more organic form, than that of the older Irish poets who wrote in English, but always to remember certain ardent ideas and high attitudes of mind which were the nation itself to our belief. . . . We were to forge in Ireland a new sword on our old traditional anvil for that great battle that must in the end re-establish the old, confident, joyous world. All the while I worked with this idea, founding societies that became quickly or slowly everything that I despised, one part of me looked on, mischievous and mocking, and the other part spoke words which were more and more unreal, as the attitude of mind became more strained and difficult.[4]

The dissatisfaction came in part from his personal defeat over the New Irish Library scheme, a proposal for the publication of a cheap popular series of Irish books to replace the Young Ireland Library. Yeats saw this scheme as a powerful agent in educating the people's taste in literature and in developing a nationalism based on a sound knowledge of Irish traditions, but it was Sir Charles Gavan Duffy who eventually gained the editorship. The first titles of the series, *The Patriot Parliament* and *The New Spirit of the Nation,* which appeared in 1893, clearly showed that Duffy intended to revive the Young Ireland movement, and the indignant Yeats withdrew from the scheme altogether, voicing his own ideals in reviews of some of the succeeding volumes and in his anthology, *A Book of Irish Verse* (1895).

There was, however, another event which deeply affected Yeats's views on the value of his native tradition and on the kind of audience he should write for. Following

the fall of Parnell and his death in 1891, political nationalism became discredited for many people in Ireland. Years
later, in a lecture on this period in Irish history, Yeats
analysed the reaction:

> Ireland was humiliated, Ireland was degraded, political
> method had been an insincere oratory, an artificial
> enthusiasm, and it had proved useless in a moral
> crisis. . . . The great political parties had broken, and the
> disputes and rivalries that had been kept down in the
> national service had come suddenly to light. . . . The old
> political poetry had ceased to be read, and our work was
> above the heads of the people.[5]

But the disillusionment opened up new avenues for
literature. Yeats saw Parnell as a sacrificial victim who
made possible the first movement of thought in modern
Ireland, a movement he described elsewhere as 'imaginative
nationalism'. 'Repelled by what had seemed the sole
reality', he wrote, 'we had turned to romantic dreaming, to
the nobility of tradition.'[6] The cultural-political cataclysm
of Parnell's death turned Yeats away from the aim of a
popular national literature as he had formerly envisaged it;
although he did not relinquish his concern for Irish
subject-matter, his poetic theory was now unhampered by
the influence of Davis's idea of Ireland; and from 1893 to
1900 he turned increasingly to London, to the English
heirs of French aestheticism, for his criteria.

1 SUBJECTS AND AUDIENCE

By 1895 Yeats was fully aware that however inadequate
his own poetry had been in reaching Davis's audience,
there was nothing to be gained in continuing that attempt.
In his introduction to *A Book of Irish Verse,* he now dis-
missed Davis as 'in the main an orator influencing men's
acts, not a poet shaping their emotions', and his criticism
became outspoken against the Young Ireland movement.[7]
At the same time, in dedicating the book to 'the small

beginning of that educated and national public, which is
our greatest need and perhaps our vainest hope', Yeats
declared that his purpose was to work for an elite, not a
popular audience. His own stories in *The Secret Rose*
(1897) were, he claimed, 'an honest attempt towards that
aristocratic, esoteric Irish literature, which has been my
chief ambition. We have a literature for the people but
nothing yet for the few.'⁸ In a letter to the editor of *The
Leader* in September 1900, Yeats argued, somewhat
fatuously, that an Irish literature in English must be
esoteric 'because the mass of the people cease to understand any poetry when they cease to understand the Irish
language, which is the language of their imaginations'; and
that such a literature 'will always be too separate from the
general life of Ireland to influence it directly.' That same
year, in his preface to the revised edition of *A Book of
Irish Verse,* he spelled out the change of aim:

> The Young Irelanders wrote to give the peasantry a
> literature in English in place of the literature they were
> losing with Gaelic, and these methods which have
> shaped the literary thought of Ireland to our time, could
> not be the same as the methods of a movement which,
> so far as it is more than an instinctive expression of
> certain moods of the soul, endeavours to create a
> reading public among the more leisured classes, which
> will preoccupy itself with Ireland and the needs of
> Ireland. . . . We cannot move these leisured classes from
> an apathy, come from their separation from the land
> they live in, by writing about Gaelic, but we may move
> them by becoming men of letters and expressing
> primary emotions and truths in ways appropriate to this
> country.⁹

In the last sentence Yeats separates himself from Douglas
Hyde's Gaelic League, a popular movement which had
gained its support out of the disillusionment and bitterness
that followed the death of Parnell, and which was to have

great practical importance in matters concerning Irish education. In an unpublished letter written to Yeats after the attacks made on the first performance of *The Countess Cathleen* in 1899, Lady Gregory showed that she agreed that the job of influencing the people as a whole could be left to Hyde's movement:

> And if your writings are a danger, why are you so abused for writing in a way hard to understand? Clearly just now your work is not directly with the masses, which would be the most directly interesting work, but that matters less as the Gaelic movement has taken up their education, and any of the fine work you do, besides having an influence on the best minds, is there ready for the time when your countrymen will dare to praise it.[10]

As Yeats later said, Douglas Hyde sought the peasant, whereas he and Lady Gregory sought the peasant imagination.[11] But in 1900 Yeats made it very clear that what he discovered about the peasant imagination was not addressed to the peasant himself.

In subject matter, 'imaginative nationalism' meant a shift from popular balladry to the material of folk-lore and legend. Although Yeats now emphasises that a poet's primary duty is 'to look into that little faltering flame that one calls oneself',[12] and that 'no writer, no artist, even though he choose Brian Borumha or St. Patrick for his subject, should try to make his work popular',[13] his concern for Ireland is still being voiced in idealistic terms. He sees folk-lore and mythology as the servant of a poetry that will re-create a 'golden age', when love of country was fastened in and irradiated by a kind of pantheism; when, Yeats argues, there was a sense of sanctity in the very landscape. He claims that Irish legends 'will some day be the themes of poets and painters in many countries, and the substance of a new romantic movement'; that they can be made a vehicle for 'that desire to be set at rest amid ideal perfection which is becoming conscious in the minds of poets.'[14] In his essay, 'The Autumn of the Body', which was an explanation and a defence of French aestheticism, Yeats went so far as to see the poet in the role of priest:

> The arts are, I believe, about to take upon their shoulders the burdens that have fallen from the shoulders of priests, and to lead us back on our journey by filling our thoughts with the essences of things, and not with things.[15]

Legends, he insists, present life 'not as it is, but as the heroic part of us, the part which desires always dreams and emotions greater than any in the world . . . hopes in secret it may become.'[16] The distinctions are important ones because barely five years later, in 1902, Yeats radically changed his theory and his practice, and advocated a language for poetry that dealt directly with life as it is, drawing its strength from things and not their 'essences'.

2 ESOTERIC IDEALISM AND THE IRISH TRADITION

> I felt my criticism would carry no weight unless I separated myself from the old gush and folly. I want people to accept my praise of Irish books as something better than mere national vanity. . . . I wrote that introduction to *A Book of Irish Verse* to convince them that we were critics and writers before all else and not heady and undiscriminating enthusiasts.[17]

Having escaped the need to view his native literature as the handmaid of the political idea which was embodied — however imperfect the art — in the verse of the Young Irelanders, by 1895 Yeats was able to take a different critical stance with regard to Irish writing, past and present. His position was forthrightly set out during that year in a letter to the editor of the Dublin *Daily Express* 27 February, in four articles on 'Irish National Literature' published in *The Bookman,* and in his introduction to *A*

Book of Irish Verse. Two factors mark this criticism. First, Yeats is now applying external standards of judgement. 'The true ambition', he wrote to the editor of *United Ireland*, 'is to make criticism as international, and litera- ture as National, as possible.'[18] In accordance with this aim, two of *The Bookman* articles are introduced by com- ments on the nature and purpose of literature which reveal the particular way Yeats interpreted the doctrine of French aestheticism. Second, he is no longer satisfied with the criteria he had formerly used to assess a literature that he had claimed was in its ballad and epic age:

> . . . and if we have not the desire for artistic perfection for an ark, the deluge of incoherence, vulgarity and triviality will pass over our heads. If we had no other symbols but the tumult of the sea, the rusted gold of the thatch, the redness of the quicken berry, and had never known the rhetoric of the platform and of the newspaper, we could do without laborious selection and rejection.[19]

In other words, Yeats no longer sees Ireland's literature in a privileged 'primitive' position; and concurrent with that changed opinion comes a revised notion of the nature of Irish tradition, which is revealed in his comments on Moore and Davis.

Both these poets had been listed along with several others, some of whom were translators, as suitable for Katharine Tynan's collection *Irish Love Songs* (1892) because, Yeats argued, their work, unlike that of English poets, was not 'literary poetry'; and he advised that 'every person who shows English influence in any way should be rejected.'[20] In 1895, however, perfunctorily dismissing Thomas Moore's work except for two poems (one of which in fact is not in conventional English metrics), Yeats declared that

It was not indeed until Callanan wrote his naive and

haunting translations from the Gaelic that anything of an honest style came into use.[21]

Quite contrary to the view he held in 1889, he now sees the tradition of the translations as being broken by the song and ballad writers who came after them. The most influential voices of the first half of the nineteenth century were, he says, Moore, Davis and Mitchel; and their common fault was that they

> ... turned away from the unfolding and developing of an Irish tradition, and borrowed the mature English methods of utterance and used them to sing of Irish wrongs or preach of Irish purposes. Their work was never wholly satisfactory, for what was Irish in it looked ungainly in an English garb and what was English was never perfectly mastered, never wholly absorbed into their being.[22]

Yeats now turns again to Callanan and chooses his work as the first distinctive expression of a truly Irish tradition in English. It is a judgement now generally corroborated by scholars in this field,[23] but Yeats was the first to make it and his reasons for doing so throw an important light on his preoccupations at that time:

> Meanwhile, Callanan, a wastrel who had wandered from place to place, from trade to trade ... had begun, or rather had expressed for the first time in English, the traditions which have moulded nearly all of modern Irish literature. While Moore's sentimental trivialities were in their first fame, he printed in Irish periodicals four translations from the Gaelic of great simplicity and charm. ... It is very difficult to describe the peculiar quality of these verses, for their quality is a new colour, a new symbol, rather than a thing of thought or form. Despite their constant clumsiness and crudity, they brought into the elaborate literature of the modern world the cold vehemence, the arid definiteness, the

tumultuous movement, the immeasurable dreaming of the Gaelic literature. Generations may pass before this tradition is mature enough in the new tongue for any to measure its full importance, but its importance to Ireland needed and needs no measuring.[24]

Having dropped the criteria applicable to a popular balladry, what strikes Yeats in Callanan has little to do with form. He does speak of 'cold vehemence' and 'arid definiteness', but these are qualities in the translations that he did not for several years recognise fully enough for them to influence his own work; at this point it was 'the immeasurable dreaming of the Gaelic literature' that caught his imagination.

It is in similar terms that the work of contemporary Irish poets is judged in Yeat's third article on Irish National Literature in *The Bookman.* Here AE (George Russell) and Douglas Hyde receive the highest praise. Because in the former's totally individual symbolism he finds 'a continual desire for union with the spirit', Yeats declares that

> No voice in modern Ireland is as beautiful to me as his . . . he, more than any, has a subtle rhythm, an emotional relation to form and colour, and a perfect understanding that the business of poetry is not to enforce opinion or expound an action, but to bring us into communion with the moods and passions which are the creative powers behind the universe.[25]

Now, the fact that Yeats in the same article, and elsewhere,[26] finds the same meanings in Hyde's translations from the Gaelic illuminates a very important feature of his critical attitudes at this date. As is clear from his comments on the rhythm of AE's verse, Yeats's principles about form are now drawn from the French and English stylists, not from Anglo-Irish balladry; but when he speaks of the Irish tradition, he is now much more concerned with *what* is being expressed than with *how*. Here is a verse he quotes from AE:

> Lights of infinite pity star the grey dusk of our day;
>   Surely here is soul; with it we have eternal breath:
> In the fire of love we live or pass by many ways
>   By unnumbered ways of dream to death.

And here is part of one of Hyde's prose translations quoted by Yeats in the same article:

> It is happy for thee, O blind man, who dost not see much of woman. Och, if thou wert to see what we see, thou wouldst be sick even as I am. It is a pity, O God, that it is not blind I was before I saw her twisted cool (hair) and her snowy body . . .

Yeats says that Hyde's *Love Songs of Connacht* (1893) express 'this emotional nature [of the Irish Celt] in its most extreme form, for . . . they seem to be continually straining to express a something which lies beyond the possibilities of expression, some vague, immeasurable emotion.' The similarity of Yeats's last phrase here to the one he used to describe 'the peculiar quality' of Callanan's poetry is no accident, for it is in Hyde's *Love Songs of Connacht* that he consistently finds evidence of the continuance of the tradition of the translations from the Gaelic. But Yeats's citing AE alongside Hyde and Callanan shows that he cannot be thinking in any way of a tradition in *form*. For Yeats during the late 1890s, what was Irish in Callanan (his 'immeasurable dreaming'), in Hyde (his 'straining to express . . . some vague, immeasurable emotion'), and in AE (his 'communion with the moods and passions') has very little to do with language at all. AE's diction is totally different from that of the two translators; and it is not until after 1900, when he has begun to look for a style based on 'common idiom', that Yeats recognises this difference and attacks AE's vagueness and imprecision.[27]

The change to 'imaginative nationalism' brought about a complete revision of Yeats's concept of popular poetry. He now declared:

> There is only one kind of good poetry, for the poetry of the coteries, which presupposes the written tradition, does not differ in kind from the true poetry of the people, which presupposes the unwritten tradition. Both are alike strange and obscure, and unreal to all who have not understanding, and both, instead of that manifest logic, that clear rhetoric of the 'popular poetry', glimmer with thoughts and images whose 'ancestors were stout and wise', 'anigh to Paradise', 'ere men yet knew the gift of corn'.[28]

In swinging away from poetry as the expression of political or moralistic opinion, Yeats set up criteria that by their nature evaded clear definition. 'It may be', he argues, 'that poetry is the utterance of desires that we can only satisfy in dreams . . . and that a spiritual world, where all dreams come true, is everything.'[29] But what Yeats had not seen was that the very translations he praised as being the embodiment of the 'Celtic spirit' relied in language on the concrete and specific, qualities which he deliberately avoided in most of the poems in *The Wind Among the Reeds* (1899). Here are parts of the many illustrations Yeats gives of the translations:

> The Erne shall be in strong flood, the hills shall be torn down, and the sea shall have red waves, and blood shall be spilled, and every mountain valley and every moor shall be on high, before you shall perish, my little black rose.

> The clouds are long above me this night. . . . Every day that comes to me is long. . . . No one in this great world is like me — a poor old man dragging stones. The clouds are long above me this night. I am the last man of the

Fianna, the great Oisin, the son of Finn, listening to the sound of bells.

The swans on the water are nine times blacker than a
    blackberry,
Since the man died from us that had pleasantness on the
    top of his fingers . . .
And since he was laid in the grave, the cold is getting the
    upper hand.

The language of the 'true poetry of the people' is not strange and obscure; it is its subject and the nature of its emotion that are the opposite of 'that clear rhetoric of the "popular poetry".'

Seeking qualities of beauty, strangeness and mystery, what one might call the subtle evidence of the soul, Yeats was led for a time to exaggerate one element of the Gaelic tradition and to ignore its matter-of-factness, its realism. It is not until after 1900 that he begins to recognise the distinctive features of Hyde's use of Anglo-Irish syntax and idiom, and to praise it for its concreteness, its lack of abstraction, its characteristics of 'living speech'. In doing so, he comes to a much clearer view of the nature of his native heritage, and develops an aesthetic which again takes its starting point from what is simple and direct, but which is this time informed by a dynamic principle: the presentation of 'the whole man . . . blood, imagination, intellect, running together'[30] by means of the spoken word.

3 BALLAD FORM IN *THE WIND AMONG THE REEDS*

In the meantime, however, Yeats's aim to create an esoteric Irish literature meant that poetry should become more elaborate and complex, and as early as 1892 his own work had already been moving in that direction. 'When I was writing the poems in . . . the section called "The Rose" ', he later noted, 'I found that I was becoming unintelligible to the young men [Davis's audience of Young

Irelanders] who had been in my thought.'[31] Nearly all the
poems in that section which were published after 1891,
and particularly those using the Rose as a symbol, were
indeed markedly 'literary', frequently carrying mystical
and occult meanings. Witness the opening of the title
poem, 'To the Rose upon the Rood of Time':

> Red Rose, proud Rose, sad Rose of all my days!
> Come near me while I sing the ancient ways:
> Cuchulain battling with the bitter tide;
> The Druid, grey, wood-nurtured, quite-eyed,
> Who cast round Fergus dreams, and ruin untold;
> And thine own sadness, whereof stars, grown old
> In dancing silver-sandalled on the sea,
> Sing in their high and lonely melody.
> Come near, that no more blinded by man's fate,
> I find under the boughs of love and hate,
> In all poor foolish things that live a day,
> Eternal beauty wandering on her way.

That is very far from a popular mode, in style or subject;
its vague allusiveness and personal mysticism contrast
sharply with the concrete evocation of the 'Irish' poems
discussed in Chapter I, which were written just a few years
earlier.

Nevertheless, for all the obscurity — deliberate or other-
wise — of Yeats's esoteric lyricism after 1891, the 1899
volume, *The Wind Among the Reeds,* did contain one or
two songs and several poems written in the ballad quatrain
where the form itself seems to have imposed a clarity on
what was said. Of the most unassuming among them, 'The
Song of the Old Mother', Yeats later stated that it was
'composed to a tune in the gapped scale'.[32] Whether or not
the Irish music played any part in controlling its diction,
this poem is a straightforward statement of the old
woman's predicament; in addition Yeats identifies his subject as Irish by using the words 'seed of the fire', which, his
note points out, is 'the Irish phrase for the little fragment

of burning turf and hot ashes which remains in the hearth from the day before'.[33] Both literal and metaphorical in meaning, this repeated phrase holds the poem together and gives it authenticity of feeling and mood.

Although it was first published in 1892, 'The Fiddler of Dooney' is placed at the end of *The Wind Among the Reeds*. In a light-hearted way it exalts the Irish song-maker above the Irish priest, though both are of the same family. It is Yeats's signature to a volume of complex poems whose aesthetic principle was to see art as an expression of the spiritual and mystical, and it is particularly appropriate for an Irish audience since both poet and priest had for centuries been part of the life of the general community in the west of Ireland where the poem is set.

With 'The Song of Wandering Aengus', however, comes a different use of simple language. Yeats says the poem was suggested to him by a Greek folk-song, and declares that the folk belief of Greece is very like that of Ireland.[34] Certainly it has a directness of statement that stands out vividly from most of the other poems in the 1899 volume:

> I went out to the hazel wood,
> Because a fire was in my head,
> And cut and peeled a hazel wand,
> And hooked a berry to a thread;
> And when white moths were on the wing,
> And moth-like stars were flickering out,
> I dropped the berry in a stream
> And caught a little silver trout.

And a different kind of link with Irish tradition is seen in the second stanza, where the vision of the 'glimmering girl' metamorphosed from the trout caught in the stream suggests the Gaelic *aisling* poem.[35] But 'The Song of Wandering Aengus' is clearly a poem of its period (first published in 1897) in that it uses symbolism as its main device: the poet promises to find the girl, who had called him by his name and then 'faded through the brightening air', and with her

> . . . pluck till time and times are done
> The silver apples of the moon,
> The golden apples of the sun.

— which in Yeats's mystical terminology means the discovery of Art represented by the embrace of the common and the kingly.[36] When Yeats again uses the vision theme, in *Cathleen ni Houlihan* (1901), its effect is powerful not only because of its timing at the very end of the play but also because it acts out in dramatically simple terms a familiar metaphor. Later, in 'Among School Children', the vision of 'a Ledean body' introduces a much more complex theme, but its meaning is carried by exact images, not by a private symbolism.

For its general structure, the method Yeats used in 'The Song of Wandering Aengus' is explained in a letter he wrote in 1899 to a contemporary Irish poet, Dora Sigerson:

> I think a kind of half ballad, half lyric, is your best manner, though I may only like this best because I think it is the kind of poem I like best myself — a ballad that gradually lifts . . . from purely circumstantial to purely lyrical writing. If you work on you are quite sure to do finer and finer work just because you write in such a simple and circumstantial way. You build up from the ground instead of starting like most writers of verse with an insincere literary language which they can apply to anything. Try, however, I think, to build about a lyric emotion. I only learnt that slowly and used to be content to tell stories. . . . One must always have lyric emotion or some revelation of beauty.[37]

Yeats's comment that he 'used to be content to tell stories' refers to the four early ballads, and bears out the criticism that they were written from the outside, their emotional

content having been imposed on stories that were merely
anecdotal. In 'The Song of Wandering Aengus', as in three
poems of the same volume which tell a story in the ballad
quatrain, Yeats uses the technique he praises in Dora
Sigerson's work: a gradual lifting 'from purely circumstantial to purely lyrical writing.' In his note to the first of
them, 'The Host of the Air', Yeats regrets not having taken
down the words as they were given him in translation from
the Gaelic poem quoted by an old woman in Ballysodare,
and the opening stanzas confirm that here there is no
direct borrowing of language:

> O'Driscoll drove with a song
> The wild duck and the drake
> From the tall and tufted reeds
> Of the drear Hart Lake.
>
> And he saw how the reeds grew dark
> At the coming of night-tide,
> And he dreamed of the long dim hair
> Of Bridget his bride.

Nevertheless, the Gaelic source of the poem does hold it
faithfully to a subject that is perfectly appropriate to Irish
folk-lore. In the original ballad, Yeats says, 'the husband
found the keeners keening his wife when he got to the
house';[38] and his own poem at first contained this detail.
Here are the last two stanzas as printed in *The Bookman* in
November 1893:

> He knew now the folk of the air,
> And his heart was blackened by dread,
> And he ran to the door of his house;
> Old women were keening the dead;
>
> But he heard high up in the air
> A piper piping away,
> And never was piping so sad;
> And never was piping so gay.

The fact that in 1899 Yeats scrapped the penultimate stanza shows him changing the nature of his source: he clearly wanted to stress the equivocal 'lyric emotion' evoked by the symbolism of the pipe music, not the stark, factual detail of the folk original.[39]

In 'The Cap and Bells', even though Yeats's style is less heavily descriptive than is generally the case in *The Wind Among the Reeds,* the 'circumstantial writing' has dwindled to the opening stanzas only, and what story there is, is purely a vehicle for symbolism. 'The Blessed' moves even closer to the prevailing tone of the volume, shown especially in its last two stanzas:

> 'O blessedness comes in the night and the day
> And whither the wise heart knows;
> And one has seen in the redness of wine
> The Incorruptible Rose,

> 'That drowsily drops faint leaves on him
> And the sweetness of desire,
> While time and the world are ebbing away
> In twilights of dew and of fire.'

In 'The Cap and Bells' a jester is in love with a queen; in 'The Blessed' a drunken man is said to be 'the blessedest soul in the world'. As is discoverable elsewhere in Yeats's early poetry, here are subjects muffled up in vague symbolism who later — in the lyrics of *The King of the Great Clock Tower* and in 'The Pilgrim' — will speak out in a language at once starkly vigorous and powerfully evocative.

The title of *The Wind Among the Reeds* was aptly chosen for here Yeats was principally concerned with the subtle expression of his own personal responses to his subject matter. In an attack on Young Ireland popular verse, he declared that the source of true poetry is 'a capricious inspiration coming with an unforeseen message out of the dim places of the mind', and quoted Maeterlinck's view that real truth is mystical, 'come out of a solitary and mysterious ideal.'[40] But he was not content merely to follow the current poetic vogue; he tried to fasten his symbolism in Irish mythology and landscape:

> I sought some symbolic language reaching far into the past and associated with familiar names and conspicuous hills that I might not be alone with the obscure impressions of the senses.[41]

It was, however, a vain attempt, for in most of the poetry written between 1892 and 1900 neither the structure of legend nor the concreteness of landscape is used to root the private symbolism firmly in form and place. Although Yeats claimed in 1901 that he had made a new style by writing about Ireland,[42] there is very little evidence of subject shaping style in *The Wind Among the Reeds;* rather it is the way the poet sees his subject that controls the way he writes about it. In the poems which make specific reference to Irish mythology or folk-lore, that subject-matter is only dimly apprehended through the prevailing mood of world-weariness and the substance of dreams, a 'Celtic Twilight' which Yeats fashioned for himself and which was not native Irish at all.[43] Even in 'The Valley of the Black Pig', a poem about the legendary prophecy of a great battle where the enemies of the Irish peasantry will be destroyed, the subject is emasculated so that the peasant speaks in the terminology shared by nearly all the other poems in that volume:

> The dews drop slowly and dreams gather: unknown
>   spears
> Suddenly hurtle before my dream-awakened eyes,
> And then the clash of fallen horsemen and the cries
> Of unknown perishing armies beat about my ears.
> We who labour by the cromlech on the shore,
> The grey cairn on the hill, when day sinks drowned
>   in dew,

Being weary of the world's empires, bow down to you,
Master of the still stars and the flaming door.

In an explanatory note appended to the poem's first printing, Yeats states: 'I have myself heard say that the girths
shall rot from the bellies of the horses, because of the few
men that shall come alive out of the valley'. It is a measure
of the way Yeats dealt with his material that such realistic
detail is entirely excluded from his poem.

  Looking back on this period in 1913, Yeats analysed the
inadequacies of the symbolist aesthetic, but he also gave an
illuminating justification of its viewpoint:

The manner of painting had changed, and we were interested in the fall of drapery and the play of light
without concerning ourselves with the meaning, the
emotion of the figure itself. How many successful
portrait-painters gave their sitters the same attention,
the same interest they might have given to a ginger-beer
bottle and an apple? and in our poems an absorption in
fragmentary sensuous beauty or detachable ideas had
deprived us of the power to mould vast material into a
single image.[44]

This analogy with impressionistic painting helps to explain
the curious divorce of style from subject in much of the
poetry of the Rhymers' Club; more importantly, it explains how in *The Wind Among the Reeds* Yeats's sole
interest in his own response to his subject matter determined the recondite nature of his references to Irish
mythology and folk-lore, and governed the way he dealt
with them.

4 THE SONGS OF RED HANRAHAN

Nothing more strikingly shows Yeats's attitude to his folk
material in 1899 than the poems supposedly spoken by
Red Hanrahan. In the *Collected Poems* they carry the
following titles: 'He reproves the Curlew', 'He remembers
Forgotten Beauty', 'A Poet to His Beloved', 'He tells of the

Perfect Beauty', 'The Secret Rose', 'Maid Quiet', and 'The Lover speaks to the Hearers of his Songs in the Coming Days', but originally each poem named Red Hanrahan (or O'Sullivan the Red, or O'Sullivan Rua) in its title. The name was taken from the famous Gaelic poet, Owen Roe O'Sullivan (1748-84), but Yeats's persona expresses attitudes totally foreign to the eighteenth century Gaelic tradition. Yeats's Red Hanrahan, along with his Aedh and his Michael Robartes, was one of the 'imaginary inhabitants' of a world situated more in Yeats's head than in Ireland, as his note to the 1899 volume points out:

> These are personages in *The Secret Rose;* but, with the exception of some of Hanrahan's and one of Aedh's poems, the poems are not out of that book. I have used them in this book more as principles of the mind than as actual personages. It is probable that only students of the magical tradition will understand me when I say that 'Michael Robartes' is fire reflected in water, and that Hanrahan is fire blown by the wind, and that Aedh . . . is fire burning by itself.[45]

Any of the poems referred to would serve as an example; here is one of the simplest of them, first published under the title, 'O'Sullivan the Red to Mary Lavell':

> I bring you with reverent hands
> The books of my numberless dreams,
> White woman that passion has worn
> As the tide wears the dove-grey sands,
> And with heart more old than the horn
> That is brimmed from the pale fire of time:
> White woman with numberless dreams,
> I bring you my passionate rhyme.
>
> ('A Poet to his Beloved')

Only one of the poems spoken by Red Hanrahan, now entitled 'The Secret Rose', draws upon Irish mythology and folk-lore, and that so allusively that Yeats's long note

on the poem is absolutely necessary to the general reader
for identification. Here Yeats attributes several of his
sources to the books of Standish O'Grady, but it was not
until 1922 that he added the comment: 'I only knew him
[Fergus, the 'proud dreaming king' in the poem] in Mr.
Standish O'Grady, and my imagination dealt more freely
with what I did know than I would approve of today'.[46]
Yeats owed nothing to O'Grady's style, which he was later
to chastise as shaped by Macaulay;[47] his poem is very much
in the predominant mode of *The Wind Among the Reeds,*
where he stamps his subject-matter with his own
romanticism:

> FAR-OFF, most secret, and inviolate Rose,
> Enfold me in my hour of hours; where those
> Who sought thee in the Holy Sepulchre,
> Or in the wine-vat, dwell beyond the stir
> And tumult of defeated dreams; and deep
> Among pale eyelids, heavy with the sleep
> Men have named beauty. Thy great leaves enfold
> The ancient beards, the helms of ruby and gold
> Of the crowned Magi; and the king whose eyes
> Saw the Pierced Hands and Rood of elder rise
> In Druid vapour and make the torches dim;
> Till vain frenzy awoke and he died; and him
> Who met Fand walking among flaming dew
> By a grey shore where the wind never blew,
> And lost the world and Emer for a kiss . . .

Entitled 'O'Sullivan Rua to the Secret Rose' in its first
printing, the poem attempts to link pagan and Christian
experience under the multifarious symbol of the Rose, invoked as a mystical force in the opening and closing lines.
The way Yeats selected his references to Irish mythology
and folk-lore, which continue throughout the poem, is in-
dicated by the detail he excludes from his picture of the
death of King Conchubar in lines 9-12. In his note to the
poem, Yeats admits that Conchubar 'did not see the
crucifix in a vision, but was told about it. He had been

struck by a ball, made out of the dried brain of a dead enemy, and hurled out of a sling'. Yeats's note continues with Keating's graphic account of the story which ends, not in a vision as the poem has it, but in Conchubar's rage at the news of the crucifixion causing the ball to start out of his head: 'and some of the brain came after it, and in that way he died.'[48] Similarly, the Cuchulain of the poem (lines 12-15) is very far from the heroic figure of Irish legend. By the time Yeats came to write his plays on the Cuchulain theme, he had relinquished the style of *The Wind Among the Reeds;* furthermore, he now not only had the 'noble writing'[49] of Lady Gregory's *Cuchulain of Muirthemne* (1902) as source material, but he also had her help in constructing the first of those plays, *On Baile's Strand.*[50]

The verses Yeats put into the mouth of Red Hanrahan in 1899 were, however, perfectly in keeping with the atmosphere created in the stories of *The Secret Rose* (1897). To turn to the Hanrahan in the title poem of *The Tower* (1928) brings perhaps the biggest shock of contrast to be found anywhere in Yeats's poetry. Here Hanrahan is described as an 'old lecher with a love on every wind', and is invoked as spokesman of the reality of the imagination, which is the poem's major theme. But the change did not begin with that poem at all; it began with a dramatically abrupt shift in Yeats's attitude to his folk material which came from the need to find a language that would be closely knit to the actual and the real, the language of a man speaking under the pressure of feelings that have their roots in the common circumstances of life. In 1904 the *Stories of Red Hanrahan* (taken from the *The Secret Rose*) were with Lady Gregory's help 'put into the common speech',[51] and Yeats specifically repudiated the language of the 1897 volume as having 'separated my imagination from life, sending my Red Hanrahan, who should have trod the same roads with myself, into some undiscoverable country.'[52]

III The True Tradition: Translations from the Gaelic

Apart from those few poems he defined as 'Irish', Yeats's early work shows very little evidence of being influenced by the translations from the Gaelic which by 1895 he was praising as the main line of his native tradition in verse written in English. When he wrote ballads like 'Moll Magee' Yeats was as far from that tradition as he was when, working several years later from new aesthetic principles, he searched in Irish folk-lore and mythology for the symbols of an esoteric lyricism. Initially he commended the translations for their personal emotion; and it is not until after 1900 that he emphasises the strength and clarity of their language, the vigour of their syntax and idiom. As can be seen from the work of translators from Callanan to Hyde, Yeats was to gain more from their tradition than he was at first aware existed in it.

1 CALLANAN, FERGUSON AND WALSH

Knowing very little Gaelic, the only way Yeats could judge the translations was to see what marked them off as different both from native English poetry and from the poetry of Irish writers who merely imitated English fashions; and although in 1895 he was more concerned with mood than with manner, it was clearly by this criterion that he claimed Callanan as the first to bring 'an honest style' into use. The original verse of J.J.Callanan (1795-1829) shows the influence of Byron, Scott and Moore, but the few translations he made from the Gaelic represent something quite different from the main work in this field available during his lifetime. Charlotte Brooke's

Reliques of Irish Poetry (1789) consisted of heroic poems,
odes, elegies and songs. While her book was the first to
bring the legendary figurès of Cuchulain and Deirdre to the
imagination of English-speaking Ireland, its main use to
subsequent translators was in the definitive Gaelic texts
supplied. The distinctive qualities of Gaelic verse, Miss
Brooke says, are its simplicity, force, dignity and rapid
energy, but how little of these she succeeds in conveying
to the English reader can be seen from this stanza from a
song called 'The Maid of the Valley':

> Have you not seen the charmer of the vale:
>   Nor heard her praise, in Love's fond accents drest? —
> Nor how that Love had turn'd my youth so pale! —
> Nor how those graces rob my soul of rest! —

Small chance there for the beginnings of an Anglo-Irish
tradition in poetry! Although Charlotte Brooke's language
is not everywhere as vapid as this, it is always that of a
stereotyped literary convention. James Hardiman's *Irish
Minstrelsy* (1831) makes very little discernible progress
from Miss Brooke's volume. His group of translators set
out to convey the spirit of the original Gaelic, but again
what we get for the most part is sophistication of sentiment and ornateness of language set in rigid English
metrics. In contrast, Callanan's 'honesty' at its best comes
up with a colloquial vocabulary and a rhythm neither of
which is quite normal usage in English verse. Here is his
translation 'The Outlaw of Loch Lene':

> O many a day have I made good ale in the glen,
> That came not of stream, or malt, like the brewing of
>   men.
> My bed was the ground, my roof, the greenwood above,
> And the wealth that I sought — one far kind glance from
>   my love.
>
> Alas! on that night when the horses I drove from the
>   field,

That I was not near from terror my angel to shield.
She stretched forth her arms, — her mantle she flung to
    the wind,
She swam o'er Loch Lene, her outlawed lover to find.

O would that a freezing sleet-winged tempest did sweep,
And I and my love were alone far off on the deep!
I'd ask not a ship, or a bark, or pinnace to save, —
With her hand round my waist, I'd fear not the wind or
    the wave.

'Tis down by the lake where the wild tree fringes its
    sides,
The maid of my heart, the fair one of Heaven resides —
I think as at eve she wanders its mazes along,
The birds to go sleep by the sweet wild twist of her
    song.

Miss Brooke pointed out in her introduction how difficult
it is to find English equivalents for the compound epithets
so common in Gaelic or for the numerous synonyms that
language provides, but Callanan finds words that are at
once effectively descriptive and unconventional. Nouns are
more important than verbs: the force of the poem depends
on their direct evocation of experience; and the syntax,
which may seem to the English ear merely awkward inversion for the sake of the rhyme — as for example in the first
line of stanzas two, three and four — gives emphasis to the
noun in a way that is characteristic of Anglo-Irish dialect
usage. The break with Charlotte Brooke is as much in
rhythm as in diction and syntax: despite the couplet
rhyme, stress is demanded by meaning rather than by the
measure of a regular prosody. And because the regular foot
is broken, as in the last line of stanzas one and four, there
is the sense of a spoken rather than a verse rhythm.

If some early Yeats seems to echo Callanan's rhythm,
that rhythm had sounded in the interim, and even more
strongly, in Ferguson. Several of his translations of Gaelic

songs which first appeared in the *Dublin University Magazine* in 1834 and were published in his *Lays of the Western Gael* (1865) show a development of the movement and measure of Callanan's verse and have the same substantival strength. Ferguson's 'The Fair Hills of Ireland' provided a pattern for what Yeats called his 'own music' in 'The Lake Isle of Innisfree'; and the same grouping of stresses, particularly at the end of the lines, controls the rhythms of his translation 'Cashel of Munster'. Here are its opening stanzas:

> I'd wed you without herds, without money, or rich
>   array,
> And I'd wed you on a dewy morning at day-dawn
>   grey;
> My bitter woe it is, love, that we are not far away
> In Cashel town, though the bare deal board were
>   our marriage-bed this day;
>
> Oh, fair maid, remember the green hill side,
> Remember how I hunted about the valleys wide;
> Time has now worn me; my locks are turn'd to grey,
> The year is scarce and I am poor, but send me not,
>   love, away!

As in Callanan, the syntax breaks across the metrical foot and, together with the concreteness of the evocation, makes the feeling vivid and genuine.

Edward Walsh (1805-50) published two volumes of translations, *Reliques of Irish Jacobite Poetry* (1844) and *Irish Popular Songs* (1847). The latter, which Yeats frequently refers to and which he drew upon for songs in his plays, gives an intimate and personal picture of Gaelic life. Walsh claims that his English versions are 'faithful, and in most instances, perfectly literal transcripts of the Irish' and that, as distinct from the practice of Brooke and Hardiman, the line measure he uses fits the tune to which the Gaelic was sung. But in view of the difficulties imposed by this sort of translation, it is not surprising that only here and there do we find lines that stand out in complete distinctiveness; and usually, as with Callanan — as indeed with Hyde when he translates into verse forms — this occurs where there is a colloquial directness of statement that needs no manipulating to match the rhyme.

When in 1888 Yeats wrote 'Love Song' (one of his 'Irish' poems), he made its mood more languid and dreamy than his source in Walsh's literal translation; the use he makes of a Gaelic song many years later is a transformation in the other direction. Here are three stanzas from Walsh's translation 'The Fair Young Child':

> My Paistin Fionn is my soul's delight —
> Her heart laughs out in her blue eyes bright;
> The bloom of the apple her bosom white,
>   Her neck like the March swan's in whiteness!
>
> Were I in our village where sports prevail,
> Between two barrels of brave, brown ale,
> My fair little sister to list my tale,
>   How jovial and happy I'd make me!
>
> In fever for nine long nights I've lain
> From lying in the hedge-row beneath the rain,
> While, gift of my bosom! I'd hop'd in vain,
>   Some whistle or call might awake ye!

Since this was a well-known song, the shift in language usage, and consequently in meaning and tone, can be observed from Hardiman through Ferguson and Walsh to Yeats. The Gaelic for the second verse quoted above is exactly the same as that found in Hardiman. This is what his translator, John D'Alton, makes of it:

> With what rapture I'd quaff it, were I in the hall
> Where feasting — and pledging — and music recall
> Proud days of my country! While she on my breast
> Would recline, my heart's twin one! and hallow the feast.

That is a courtly picture. Ferguson's language is more vigorous, less genteel than Walsh's, particularly by virtue of the refrain. His third and fourth stanzas are as follows:

> Were I in the town, where's mirth and glee
> Or 'twixt two barrels of barley bree,
> With my fair Pastheen on my knee,
> 'Tis I would drink to her pleasantly!
>   Then, Oro, come with me! come with me!
>   come with me!
>   Oro, come with me! brown girl, sweet!
>   And oh! I would go through snow and sleet,
>   If you would come with me, brown girl sweet!
>
> Nine nights I lay in longing and pain,
> Betwixt two bushes beneath the rain,
> Thinking to see you, love, once again;
> But whistle and call were all in vain!
>   Then, Oro, come with me! come with me! . . .

The last stanza of Yeats's song, 'My Paistin Finn', first printed in his play *The Pot of Broth* in 1922, shows how closely he followed Ferguson:

> Nine nights I lay in longing sore
> Between two bushes under the rain;
> Thinking to meet my love once more
> I cried and whistled but vain, all vain.

Yeats's final version of this song makes further changes in the nature of the relationship. Here is its opening stanza:

> My Paistin Finn is my sole desire,
> And I am shrunken to skin and bone,
> For all my heart has had for its hire
> Is what I can whistle alone and alone.
>   *Oro, oro!*
> *Tomorrow night I will break down the door.*

This is a bare statement of physical need (note the shift in

the first line from Walsh's 'my soul's delight' — Ferguson
has 'my heart's delight' — to Yeats's 'my sole desire')
which, for all the lustiness of the refrain carries with it a
wistful mood that entirely escapes sentimentality. It gives
a foretaste of the tone of the 'Crazy Jane' poems; and, like
many of Yeats's late songs and ballads, its effects are
created by a concrete specification which is typical of
Anglo-Irish dialect usage.

The only distinction Yeats makes among Walsh's translations is between the mood of 'pastoral aspiration' of the
source for his own poem 'Love Song' and the songs he calls
'passionate and wild'.[1] In fact, Walsh's work reveals considerable variety, from simple lyrics to an *aisling* like 'The
Vision of John McDonnell', an allegory in which the genius
of Ireland impersonated by the Queen of Faery leads the
poet through the mythological topography of the country.
Such poems in Walsh's collection support the point made
by Daniel Corkery in *The Hidden Ireland* (1925) that the
'academic' work of the Irish poets found its way into
popular song.[2] Yeats's description of Walsh's translations
is, however, borne out in that almost all of them are written from a personal standpoint: they are lyrical pieces that
never go beyond the expression of a single state of feeling.
There is no resolution of that feeling, no moralising of it,
and rarely any subtle change within it. Even in the most
complex of the forms, the *aisling,* the device lends itself to
the lyrical since political meanings are disguised under the
poet's distress for or praise of a maiden who is Ireland.

2 JAMES CLARENCE MANGAN

What Yeats consistently finds in Mangan is an intensifica-
tion of the personal, which he attributes to the desolation
and disappointment of the poet's life: 'outer things were
only to him mere symbols to express his own inmost and
desperate heart.'[3] There is no doubt about Yeats's estima-
tion of the importance of Mangan's poetry, and he judges
it exactly in terms of how the man is seen through his

work. As an epigraph to his first article on him,[4] Yeats quotes these lines from a translation Mangan made of Schiller's 'Die Ideale', entitled 'The Unrealities':

> All my divinities have died of grief,
> And left me wedded to the rude and real.

— and goes on to say: 'In all he wrote there was a sort of intensity, not merely of the intellectual or of the aesthetic nature, but of the whole man.'

Mangan's work, like that of the other translators, was seen by Yeats after 1893 as a contrast to the political poetry of the Young Irelanders. In his introduction to *A Book of Irish Verse* Yeats stresses that Mangan's style was formed before the Young Ireland movement began 'and for this reason perhaps he was always able to give sincere expression to the mood which he had chosen, the only sincerity literature knows of'. Undoubtedly, Mangan's own temperament must have guided his selection of the Gaelic poems he translated: he chooses laments more frequently than songs, but different as his poems are from Walsh's translations — because they convey a harsher reality in a style at once more astringent and nervously intense — they belong to the same tradition in that they are direct expressions of a state of feeling and their purpose is solely to describe it.

The terms 'lyrical intensity' and 'passion' recur constantly in Yeats's assessment of Mangan's qualities as a translator, but there was also more art in his work than Yeats was prepared to recognise. In particular, two features of Mangan's translations can be seen as prefiguring developments that were to occur in Yeats's own style. The first concerns a combination of the simple and traditional with the complex, and its most striking example is seen in Mangan's most famous translation, 'Dark Rosaleen'. Here he describes Rosaleen's 'holy delicate white hands', speaks of her as 'My virgin flower, my flower of flowers', and his refrain, 'My Dark Rosaleen' is itself traditional. But then, quite untypically of folk poetry as it is understood in the Anglo-Scots tradition, he brings in a word that concentrates feeling and thought in both sound and meaning:

> O! the Erne shall run red
> With redundance of blood.

In accordance with Mangan's general practice as a translator, this is a free rendering of the original lines in the seventeenth century Gaelic poem 'Roisin Dubh' (The Little Black Rose). But it was Mangan's version that became so enormously popular: the audience that read the translations from the Gaelic was schooled to appreciate a poetry that was more sophisticated than Yeats would admit when he was arguing for the primitive, balladic virtues of his native heritage in literature. And it was many years before he was able to use in his own poetry that combination of simple diction and the complex word which, as in such lines as:

> I spit into the face of Time
> That has transfigured me.
> ('The Lamentation of the Old Pensioner', 1925)

or as in:

> I offer to love's play
> My dark declivities.
>> ('Parting', 1929)

or in:

> There's not a bird of day that dare
> Extinguish that delight.
>> ('A Last Confession', 1929)

became one of the marks of his mature style.

Although many of Mangan's translations from the Gaelic are held to be adaptations, paraphrases or improvisations, the fact remains that Yeats accepted them as evidence of the Gaelic tradition; indeed it could be argued

that they are an exaggeration of it, for the personality of
Mangan is sometimes too stridently heard in his verse. D.J.
O'Donoghue, who edited a far from complete edition of
Mangan's poems in 1904, claims however that in
'O'Hussey's Ode to the Maguire' Mangan kept 'strikingly
close to his original'.[5] That original was written by Ó
Heoghusa (1570-1612), a professional poet who had
attended one of the Bardic schools which had a long tradition in Ireland. Up to the end of the seventeenth century
these schools gave a rigorous literary training to poets who
then went out to take up positions of power and importance in the houses of Gaelic chieftains. According to James
Carney, a distinguished present-day Gaelic scholar, Ó
Heoghusa's relationship with 'the Maguire' of the poem
was even more intense than was commonly the case between poet and patron.[6] Certainly Mangan's translation,
which Yeats claimed 'must live for generations through
sheer passion',[7] gives evidence of this. Its subject is a very
personal lament for the plight of the chieftain of Clan
Darry, a plight seen in metaphorical terms of his totally
desolate exposure to a bitter storm which has engulfed the
land. The most striking features of Mangan's technique are
that he never deviates from his subject throughout fifteen
stanzas; that he maintains the sense of immediacy by the
interplay of vivid description of the storm with recurring
emphasis on the poet's identification with his hero: a
dramatisation that comes from the concentration on his
predicament; and that the stanzas move with such syntactical vigour that the rhyme, which helps the beat and pitch
of the lament, rarely seems forced, and meaning is not
sacrificed to accommodate it. The poem is too long to be
quoted in full; these lines are representative:

> Though he were even a wolf ranging the round green
>   woods,
> Though he were even a pleasant salmon in the
>   unchainable sea,

Though he were a wild mountain eagle, he could scarce
    bear, he,
This sharp, sore sleet, these howling floods.

Large, large affliction unto me and mine it is,
That one of his majestic bearing, his fair, stately form,
Should thus be tortured and o'erborne — that this
    unsparing storm
Should wreak its wrath on head like his!

And though frost glaze tonight the clear dew of his eyes,
And white ice-gauntlets glove his fine fair fingers o'er,
A warm dress is to him that lightning garb he ever wore,
The lightning of the soul, not skies.

AVRAN

Hugh marched to the fight — I grieved to see him so
    depart;
And lo! tonight he wanders frozen, rain-drenched, sad,
    betrayed,
But the memory of the limewhite mansions his right
    hand hath laid
In ashes, warms the hero's heart!

As in his translation of the 'Lament for the Princes of
Tyrone and Tyrconnell', which is built upon a series of
conditional clauses, Mangan has here gone a long way
towards achieving 'a powerful and passionate syntax, and a
complete co-incidence between stanza and period',[8] which
Yeats defined in 1937 as his own aim. The poem has
power because of its clausal repetition, and it has passion
because the energy of its thought elicits sense: the syntax
is the feeling.

    Mangan's poetry contains one further distinctive feature
which Yeats was unable to draw upon in the 1890s because his symbolist aesthetics led him in a different direction: his use of the colloquial. Here are two stanzas from
Mangan's translation 'The Woman of Three Cows':

See where Momonia's heroes lie, proud Owen More's
    descendants,
'Tis they that won the glorious name, and had the grand
    attendants!
If *they* were forced to bow to Fate, as every mortal
    bows,
Can *you* be proud, can *you* be stiff, my Woman of
    Three Cows! . . .

Now, there you go! You still, of course, keep up your
    scornful bearing,
And I'm too poor to hinder you; but, by the cloak I'm
    wearing,
If I had but *four* cows myself, even though you were my
    spouse,
I'd thwack you well to cure your pride, my Woman of
    Three Cows!

The colloquial address vividly invokes the presence of the
woman being upbraided and falls with natural ease into the
line length. It has been noted[9] that Yeats picked up a
phrase from this poem for his 'Crazy Jane talks with the
Bishop': 'A woman can be proud and stiff/When on love
intent'; more important than such direct borrowings, however, is the example set by Mangan. Yeats eventually worked
out for himself a style which by what he called the 'natural
momentum' of its syntax and idiom could carry 'any
amount of elaborate English',[10] but a model was already
there in Mangan's translations from the Gaelic, whose subjects and spirit were so suited to his temperament as a man
and as a poet.

3 DOUGLAS HYDE

Douglas Hyde (1860-1949) was for Yeats the most important of the nineteenth century translators from the Gaelic
because his consistent use of Anglo-Irish dialect directly

influenced the poet's theory and practice. Other than Hyde,
none of Yeats's early contemporaries in Ireland saw dialect
as a viable literary medium, principally because of its distortion by both playwrights and novelists in the comic
portrayal of Irish character. In the essay 'J.M. Synge and the
Ireland of His Time', Yeats recalled that as a boy he was
'often troubled and sorrowful because Scottish dialect was
capable of noble use, but the Irish of obvious roystering
humour only'.[11] And in his own selection of stories about
Irish life, he rigorously excluded anything that had 'a touch
of the Handy Andy stage Irishman — a creature half schemer
half dunce, with little truth to nature about him'.[12] Since its
purpose was most often comic exaggeration, the kind of
writing Yeats refers to was very far from being an accurate
representation of Anglo-Irish dialect; its stock-in-trade was
the ludicrous misspelling of words combined with set
patters of phraseology, few of them authentic.

Hyde was the first to remove the stigma of farce from
the use of dialect, and Yeats was quick to recognise and
applaud his achievement. In 1891 he praised the 'perfect
style'[13] of Hyde's translations of Gaelic folk-tales in *Beside
the Fire* (1890); and Hyde's fidelity to the syntax and
idiom of peasant speech in this work would have provided
genuine illustration for Yeats's ideas at that time about a
truly native, simple and direct use of English, but he failed
to press home his argument with Hyde as his example. His
advice never got beyond the vague statement that translations should be made 'in English which shall have an in-
definable Irish quality of rhythm and style'.[14] Between
1895 and 1900, when he had completely changed his concept of the role literature should play in Ireland, the
models he gave for her writers were English literary figures.
Ireland, he felt, could not have a Burns but she could have
a Shelley, and a prose like that of Meredith, Pater and
Ruskin.[15] He did not seem to realise that the very 'clumsi-
ness and crudity' he found in Callanan's translations was
the basis of that 'honest style' he praised in him, a style

which sometimes veered into the rhythm and syntax of Anglo-Irish dialect but which seemed awkward in the alien dress of English verse forms. And when during this period he spoke so highly of Hyde's translations, he did not see Hyde's much more accomplished use of dialect as a potential language for poetry because he was concerned with moods and emotion not with modes of expression.

But Yeats soon became dissatisfied with an aesthetic dedicated to 'states of mind, lyrical moments, intellectual essences.'[16] He had barely finished writing essays (in *Ideas of Good and Evil*) in support of his theories when he repudiated them. In 'The Autumn of the Body', Yeats had seen the preoccupation with things in poets from Homer to Shakespeare as a betrayal of the true subject of poetry: the artist as priest should, he said, 'fill our thoughts with the essences of things, not with things'. In another essay, the 'lyrical and meditative ecstasies' of Robert Bridges' verse are preferred to the 'vivacity of common life' found in Shakespeare.[17] By 1903 there is a complete about-face: Yeats tells John Quinn that *Ideas of Good and Evil* 'is too lyrical, too full of aspirations after remote things, too full of desires.'[18] He found he had 'without knowing it . . . come to care for nothing but impersonal beauty';[19] furthermore, the language used was too elaborate:

> Yet those delighted senses, when I had got from them all that I could, left me discontented. Impressions that needed so elaborate a record did not seem like the handiwork of those careless old writers one imagines squabbling over a mistress, or riding on a journey, or drinking round a tavern fire, brisk and active men.[20]

From this point on, Yeats's aim is exactly that 'vivacity of common life' he had so recently scorned:

> In literature, partly from the lack of that spoken word which knits us to normal man, we have lost in personality, in our delight in the whole man — blood, imagination, intellect, running together . . .[21]

He could not find that spoken word in the verse of contemporary English poets, but he could and did find it in Anglo-Irish dialect. Instead of using vague terms like 'the immortal moods . . . the true builders of nations', instead of seeking in Gaelic lyricism the mournful or the sorrowful or 'the continual straining to express a something which lies beyond the possibility of expression',[22] soon after 1900 Yeats begins to write about the solidity and vitality of Gaelic poetry; of the sensitivity of the Irish to the reality of things seen, where everything present to the mind is present to the senses;[23] and he now specifically chooses Hyde's Anglo-Irish dialect as a medium for such expression:

> It is the only good English spoken by any large number of Irish people today, and we must found good literature on a living speech. . . . One can write well in that country idiom without much thought about one's words; the emotion will bring the right word itself, for there everything is old and everything alive and nothing common or threadbare . . . Let us get back in everything to the spoken word. . . . But when we go back to speech let us see that it is the idiom either of those who have rejected, or of those who have never learned, the base idioms of the newspapers.[24]

Yeats insisted that the modern vices of abstraction and generalisation were 'made by minds that would grasp what they have never seen',[25] and the pre-eminent virtue of 'the dialect' for him was that it dealt with life. George Moore quotes him as saying that it was 'struck out of life itself'; and that 'It is through the dialect that one escapes from abstract words, back to the sensation directly inspired by the thing itself'.[26] When in 1902 Yeats advocated the literary use of Anglo-Irish dialect, what he was looking for was not so much a new vocabulary as a way of using words that vividly revealed the speaker's own experience; that is why he defined the quality he sought as 'personality, the breath of men's mouths'.[27]

Such words are exactly what Yeats found in Hyde's *Love Songs of Connacht* (1893). He said: 'The prose parts of that book were to me . . . the coming of a new power into literature'.[28] Here is Hyde's literal translation of a poem called 'If I were to go West':

> If I were to go west, it is from the west I would not
>   come,
> On the hill that was highest, 'tis on it I would stand,
> It is the fragrant branch I would soonest pluck,
> And it is my own love I would quickest follow.
>
> My heart is as black as a sloe,
> Or as a black coal that would be burnt in a forge,
> As the sole of a shoe upon white halls,
> And there is great melancholy over my laugh.
>
> My heart is bruised, broken,
> Like ice upon the top of water,
> As it were a cluster of nuts after their breaking,
> Or a young maiden after her marrying.
>
> My love is the colour of the blackberries,
> And the colour of the raspberry on a fine sunny day.
> Of the colour of the darkest heath-berries of the
>   mountain,
> And often has there been a black head upon a bright
>   body.
>
> Time it is for me to leave this town,
> The stone is sharp in it, and the mould is cold;
> It was in it I got a voice (blame), without riches
> And a heavy word from the band who back-bite.
>
> I denounce love; woe is she who gave it
> To the son of yon woman, who never understood it.
> My heart in my middle, sure he has left it black,
> And I do not see him on the street or in any place.

These songs avoid any sort of vagueness of mood because
the things named have a direct impact on the poet's feelings; the energy that informs the starkness and intensity of
such poetry comes from direct personal involvement. The
sense of alienation in the penultimate stanza is conveyed in
terms of actual experience; and the same emphasis on the
concrete and specific presents with graphic force the picture of death in another song, 'The Brown Blackthorn':

> I am done with you, until a narrow coffin be made for
> me,
> And till the grass shall grow, after that, up through my
> middle.

A similar immediacy is seen in these lines:

> My love, oh! she is my love, The woman who is most for
> destroying me; Dearer is she from making me ill Than
> the woman would be for making me well. She is my
> treasure, Oh! she is my treasure, The woman of the grey
> (?) eye (she) like the rose, A woman who would not
> place a hand beneath my head, A woman who would
> not be with me for gold. She is my affection, Oh! she is
> my affection, The woman who left no strength in me; A
> woman who would not breathe a sigh after me, A
> woman who would not raise a stone at my tomb. . .

The syntactical repetition here, with the emphasis on the
noun 'woman' and the singling out of separate actions each
immediately relevant to the feeling being expressed, is
typical of Hyde's prose in this volume. Simplifying the
history of the translations, Yeats said in his preface to the
Dun Emer Press edition of' *Love Songs of Connacht* in
1904: 'There have been other translators but they had a
formal eighteenth century style, that took what Dr. Hyde
would call "the sap and pleasure" out of simple thought
and emotion'.[29]
The theory of poetry as the voice of personality expressed through the spoken word became Yeats's solution

to the problem of how to unite thought and feeling. Looking back in 1913, he explained:

> Of recent years instead of 'vision', meaning by vision the intense realisation of a state of ecstatic emotion symbolised in a definite imagined region, I have tried for more self-portraiture. I have tried to make my work convincing with a speech so natural and dramatic that the hearer would feel the presence of a man thinking and feeling.

At the beginning of the century considerable experiment was needed before Yeats could 'think in the marrow bone', but in the literal translations of Hyde's *Love Songs of Connacht,* as in the commentary which links the poems in that volume, Yeats had the example of a dialect which was written as it was spoken, and in which he claimed 'the emotion will bring the right word itself'; its presentation of 'the whole man' was inevitably in simple terms, but it was a beginning: Yeats had found a style where the unity he aimed for existed.

IV Yeats's Debt to Anglo-Irish Dialect*

In declaring that evocation of feeling must be founded on the reality of things named — 'the sensation directly inspired by the thing itself' — Yeats was in the forefront of twentieth century critical opinion. Just such a principle was to inform, separately and in different ways, the poetic theory of Ezra Pound and T. S. Eliot. But when Yeats first wrote about Anglo-Irish idiom as a model for the spoken word in literature, although he mentioned its syntax ('turns of phrase out of the Gaelic'),[1] he did not understand how that syntax contributes to the concreteness which is such a marked characteristic of dialect usage. What distinguishes Yeats's theory from Pound's and Eliot's is the fact that it is based on a living speech whose syntax lays greater emphasis on the noun than is normally found in standard English.

Professor P. L. Henry's text, *An Anglo-Irish Dialect of North Roscommon* (1957), gives ample evidence of the substantival character of the dialect he describes. Here is a small selection of the examples he provides, together with an abbreviation of his commentary on them:

1   Anglo-Irish dialect specifies more concretely than standard English:

'Bridget lost the breath' — Bridget died.
'Not a man nor a woman of them would know' — None of them would know.

*There are of course numerous Anglo-Irish dialects. To avoid linguistic discriminations which are beyond the scope of this book, I have accepted Yeats's general reference to 'the dialect'.

2   Nominal groups are preferred to simple pronouns, adverbs and conjunctions:
'What way?' — How?; 'What man?' — Who?; 'What's the cause?' — Why?

3   A highly developed prepositional system helps create the substantival cast of the sentence, and can take over adjectival, adverbial, and even verbal functions. Hence, the most varied relations can be expressed substantivally:
'What name did they put on 'im?' — What did they call him?
'The weight was with him' — He was heavy.
'It went to the heart in him' — He felt it very deeply.
'There's no loss on him' — He has nothing to complain about.

4   The gerund is predominantly substantival in character:
'I was at the leaving down of the first stone' — I was present when the first stone was being laid.

5   Predication by means of 'it's', ''twas' (and variants) gives direct prominence to the chief burden of the speaker's thoughts:
'It's at home she should be' — She should be at home.[2]
(In standard English emphasis in such sentences is carried by voice stress only, whereas in Anglo-Irish dialect it is controlled by word order: 'It's herself should be at home' — *She* should be at home.)

6   Several other devices, used for emphasis, which give prominence to the noun:

(*a*)   Use of 'what . . . but', in interrogative form, to make an emphatic statement:
'He was bringin' a creel of potatoes, an' the next thing what was it but an ass-foal' — i.e. the creel of potatoes changed into an ass-foal.
'The next day what landed down but two guards' — . . . two policemen arrived on the scene.

(*b*)   Use of demonstrative 'that' in emphasis:
'That's the boy does know well' — He's the one who does know well.
'That's the flour that scalded me' — The flour in question caused me serious annoyance.

(*c*)   Use of what Henry calls· a grammatically empty 'there':
'There went four carts of tinkers down the road' — Four carts of tinkers went . . .

(*d*)   Use of inversion for emphasis or greater prominence:
'There's where the cheers and the shouts would be'.[3]

In giving such emphasis to the noun, the syntax of this speech lends itself. to the description of what is concrete and actual. Its verbal system serves similar ends by using tense sequences which are not found in standard English and which most commonly· express a state of being, of actuality, of fact. The following examples are taken from P. L. Henry's text:

1   The use of the 'expanded present' tense for standard English 'inclusive' or 'expanded' perfect tense:
'He's workin' these years on it' — He has worked (or, He has been working) for years on it.

2   The use of future tense for standard English conditional tense, and of past tense for future eventuality:
Context: Do you see that bird flying across the hill? I wonder how far he can fly without stopping?
Reply: 'He'll fly on to Keadue before he stopped' — It would (be able to) fly as far as Keadue without stopping.

P. L. Henry comments on this example: 'In "before he stopped" the eventuality of stopping is relegated to the past, the sphere of fact. This is the essential point. "He'll fly" (rather than "he would fly") is used because it is correspondingly definite and actual.'

3   The use of two forms not found in standard English for the past tense:

(*a*) To be + after + ing: 'He is after writing a letter' — He has (just) written a letter.

(*b*) To have + obj + participal: 'He has it written'; 'He has a drop taken' — He was drunk.

P. L. Henry notes that in (*a*) the construction is based upon a static interpretation of action and that its function is to report the conclusion of an action by referring to a state initiated by the conclusion of this action; in (*b*) Henry points to a clear preoccupation with state, the sense of action being practically absent from the participial form (cf. 'written' and 'taken'), which is adjectival in nature.[4]

Wherever else they may occur — and some of them can be found in other dialects — these structures are characteristic of Anglo-Irish speech as Professor Henry recorded it in the mid 1940s. Its syntax is recognisably that on which Lady Gregory and Synge built for their different literary purposes, and which is most faithfully recorded in the work of Douglas Hyde. Yeats said that 'the dialect' never became his art, but he admitted that he owed much to its example:

> I found myself continually testing both my verse and my prose by translating it into dialect. I had tried in vain to rid my style of modern romantic convention ... and if I succeed[ed] at last ... it was partly, perhaps mainly through my preoccupation with peasant speech.[5]

The substantival structure of that peasant speech forced Yeats to see clearly what he was writing about; and the habit of mind evinced by that structure, which fastens on the vividly evocative, influenced his way of recording experience.

1 STORIES OF RED HANRAHAN

Although the discovery of Anglo-Irish dialect as a literary medium belongs to Hyde, it was Lady Gregory who became Yeats's guide to its use. In a note written in 1925, which now prefaces the volume *Mythologies,* Yeats comments:

> The *Stories of Red Hanrahan* . . . were, as first published, written in that artificial, elaborate English so many of us played with in the 'nineties', and I had come to hate them. When I was changing the first story . . . I asked Lady Gregory's help. We worked together . . . till all had been put into that simple English she had learned from her Galway countrymen, and the thought had come closer to the life of the people. If their style has merit now, that merit is mainly hers.

Brief examples from the first edition and from the re-written edition of these stories illustrate what changes of style occurred. First of all, here is a passage which is entirely omitted from the 1904 edition of the story 'The Twisting of the Rope'. The 1897 edition of the story opens as follows:

> There is a moment at twilight in which all men look handsome, all women beautiful, and day by day as he wandered slowly and aimlessly he passed deeper and deeper into that Celtic twilight in which heaven and earth so mingle that each seems to have taken upon itself some shadow of the other's beauty. It filled his soul with a desire for he knew not what, it possessed his body with a thirst for unimagined experiences . . .⁶

— and so it goes on for another twenty lines or more. The fanciful embroidering of that 'undiscoverable country' Yeats later referred to is plain enough: the style is characterised by deliberate vagueness and imprecision of mood. In its re-written form the story presents a more down-to-earth picture of the 'rough clad peasant': what he feels is

evoked by the details of his experience, not by an encum-
brance of 'Celtic Twilight' dreams.

The next two examples show Yeats expanding on his
original material in order to particularise what he is describing. Here is the 1897 version of an incident in the
story 'Kathleen the Daughter of Houlihan and Hanrahan
the Red':

> He accepted her offer cheerfully enough for he was tired
> of wandering, and desired domestic peace and women to
> listen to the tale of his troubles and to comfort him.[7]

And the 1904 version:

> Hanrahan was well pleased to settle down with them for
> a while, for he was tired of wandering; and since the day
> he found the little cabin fallen in, and Mary Lavelle
> gone from it, and the thatch scattered, he had never
> asked to have any place of his own; and he had never
> stopped long enough in any place to see the green leaves
> come where he had seen the old leaves wither, or to see
> the wheat harvested where he had seen it sown. It was a
> good change for him to have shelter from the wet, and a
> fire in the evening-time, and his share of food put on the
> table without the asking.[8]

In the 1897 version of 'The Curse of Hanrahan the Red',
Yeats describes Hanrahan's realisation that he is growing
old as follows:

> But he went towards the Townland of the Bridge with
> his eyes on the white dust, stooping and seeming an old
> man indeed.[9]

The 1904 version of the story relies on specific detail to
evoke an acute awareness of debility:

> And he thought of the stiffness of his joints when he
> first rose of a morning, and the pain in his knees after
> making a journey, and it seemed to him as if he was

come to be a very old man, with cold in the shoulders
and speckled shins and his wind breaking and he himself
withering away . . . and it is old and broken he looked
going home that day with the stoop in his shoulders and
the darkness in his face.[10]

In each case the re-writing of the stories makes for clarity
and emphasis. The change was so striking that in itself it
provided a model for at least one contemporary writer. In
an unpublished letter to Lady Gregory about the fifth
volume of his *Collected Works* which came out in 1908,
Yeats noted with obvious pleasure:

Did I tell you that Masefield told me that a comparison
which he made between the style of the first and the
later versions [of the *Stories of Red Hanrahan*] caused
him to alter his own style completely? It taught him to
make his style simpler and stronger. He added 'modern
style is like a steaming marsh, full of rank weeds' or
some such phrase.[11]

2 SONGS IN THE PLAYS

After 1900, Yeats's choice of traditional Irish songs for his
plays gives clear indication of the changes he was determined to bring about in his own verse. Writing to AE
about the latter's collection of Irish lyrics entitled *New
Songs* (1904), he commented:

The dominant mood in many of them is one I have
fought in myself and put down. In my *Land of Heart's
Desire* and in some of my lyric verse of that time, there
is an exaggeration of sentiment and sentimental beauty
which I have come to think unmanly. . . . We possess
nothing but the will and we must never let the children
of vague desires breathe upon it nor the waters of sentiment rust the terrible mirror of its blade. I fled from

some of this new verse you have gathered as from much verse of our day, knowing that I fled that water and that breath.[12]

One example from AE's collection will suffice to illustrate what Yeats was talking about. Here is a stanza from 'The Twilight People' by Seamus O'Sullivan:

> And I am old, and in my heart at your calling
> Only the old dead dreams a-fluttering go.
> As the wind, the forest wind, in its falling
> Sets the withered leaves a-fluttering to and fro.

That is extremely diluted Yeats of the mid nineties, and one can turn for its model to the only song in *The Land of Heart's Desire* (1894) which is, as Yeats describes the play itself, 'the call of the heart, the heart seeking its own dream':[13]

> The wind blows out of the gates of the day,
> The wind blows over the lonely of heart,
> And the lonely of heart is withered away.
> While the faeries dance in a place apart,
> Shaking their milk-white feet in a ring,
> Tossing their milk-white arms in the air;
> For they hear the wind laugh and murmur and sing
> Of a land where even the old are fair,
> And even the wise are merry of tongue;
> For I heard a reed of Coolaney say,
> 'When the wind has laughed and murmured and sung
> The lonely of heart is withered away!'

Yeats openly acknowledges Lady Gregory's help in writing *Cathleen ni Houlihan* (1902), whose title was inspired by a song written by the eighteenth century Gaelic poet Blind William Heffernan, and the change of style from the earlier play is nowhere more marked than in the songs used. Cathleen ni Houlihan, the old woman who is Ireland, sings the following song about those who have died for her:

> I will go cry with the woman,
> For yellow-haired Donough is dead,
> With a hempen rope for a neckcloth,
> And a white cloth on his head, —
>
> I am come to cry with you, woman,
> My hair is unwound and unbound;
> I remember him ploughing his field,
> Turning up the red side of the ground,
> And building his barn on the hill
> With the good mortared stone;
> O! we'd have pulled down the gallows
> Had it happened in Enniscrone!

The two songs differ widely in mood and meaning, the latter's impact coming from the vividly concrete and specific. Yeats said that it was suggested to him 'by some old Gaelic folk-song',[14] a source which has recently been identified by Michael Yeats.[15] The next song in the same play may not have a Gaelic origin, but it is written in a similar vein, its repetitive structure gaining in context a powerful rhetorical appeal:

> Do not make a great keening
> When the graves have been dug tomorrow.
> Do not call the white-scarfed riders
> To the burying that shall be tomorrow.
>
> Do not spread food to call strangers
> To the wakes that shall be tomorrow
> Do not give money for prayers
> For the dead that shall die tomorrow.
>
> They shall be remembered for ever,
> They shall be alive for ever,
> They shall be speaking for ever,
> The people shall hear them for ever.

None of the traditional songs Yeats used in his plays shows the sort of qualities he attributed to Irish folk literature in the late 1890s; their virtues are those of direct emphatic address, substantival evocation, and a total lack of sentimentality. It is in such terms that some of these songs herald Yeats's style in *Words for Music Perhaps* and in some of the ballads of *Last Poems*; and it is not merely coincidence that the old woman, 'Cracked Mary', whom Yeats names as his source for the song in *The Pot of Broth*,[16] written in 1902, is a precursor of 'Crazy Jane'. Here is the second stanza of the song:

> I wish you were dead, my gay old man,
> I wish you were dead, my gay old man,
> > I wish you were dead
> > And a stone at your head,
> So as I'd marry poor Jack the journeyman.

Yeats had met this kind of bluntness as early as 1893 in Hyde's *Love Songs of Connacht* — for example, in the following stray verse from that volume:

> Oh! dear little mother, give him myself;
> Give him the cows and the sheep altogether.
> Go yourself a-begging alms,
> And do not go west or east to look for me.[17]

—but he was at that time reading the translations from a restricting aesthetic viewpoint.

Although Yeats did not use many folk-songs for his plays, several others can be identified as sharing the same tradition of blunt realism. The following was included in Yeats's *A Book of Irish Verse* and later appeared in *On Baile's Strand* (1903), sung by The Fool with telling ironic effect to Cuchulain and the Blind Man after the former has unwittingly killed his own son:

> When you were an acorn on the tree-top,
> > Then was I an eagle-cock;
> Now that you are a withered old block,
> > Still am I an eagle-cock.

Another song Yeats used merely as repartee in *The Uni-corn from the Stars*:

> Three that are watching my time to run,
> The worm, the Devil, and my son,
> To see a loop around their neck,
> It's that would make my heart to lep!

The play was written and first performed in 1907. The year before Douglas Hyde had printed the following literal translation from the Gaelic in his *Religious Songs of Connacht*:

> Three there are watching for my death
> Though they are always with me(?)
> It is a pity they are not hanged with a gad
> The Devil, the Children, and the Worm.[18]

As a last illustration of how Yeats's choice of native Irish songs for his plays indicates the way his own stylistic preferences developed, there is an instance of his replacing one folk-song by another. The first editions of *The Pot of Broth* contained the following song called 'The Spouse of Naoise', which Yeats said he had adapted from Walsh's *Irish Popular Songs*:

> The Spouse of Naoise, Erin's woe,
> Helen and Venus long ago
> Their charms would fade, their fame would flee
> Beside mo gradh, mo stor, machree,
> > My Sibby O!
>
> Her eyes are gray like morning dew,
> Her curling hair falls to her shoe,
> The swan is blacker than my nail,
> Beside my Queen, My Granuaile,
> > My Sibby O![19]

In 1922 Yeats replaced this song with 'My Paistin Finn', whose sources are quite clearly in Ferguson and Walsh. It

suffices here to quote one of its stanzas from the final
printing:

> What is the good of a man and he
> Alone and alone with a speckled shin?
> I would that I drank with my love on my knee,
> Between two barrels at the inn,
>   *Oro, oro*!
> *Tomorrow night I will break down the door.*

This stanza gives an example — fairly rare in Yeats's poetry
— of a common feature of Anglo-Irish dialect syntax
(which was not in either of his sources) used frequently by
Hyde, Lady Gregory and Synge, which P. L. Henry describes as the 'co-ordinative use of "and" ';[20] the sense of
the spoken voice is further enhanced by the interrogative
opening and the concrete specification ('speckled shin'
vividly conveys the idea of inactivity in front of the fire,
and is usually applied to old men). The vigour of this song
contrasts strangely with the vapid story of the play.

The change Yeats made in Aleel's song from *The Countess Cathleen* shows that his own style without native
models was working in the same direction. The 1890s'
mood is plain in an early edition of the play:

> Impetuous heart, be still be still;
> Your sorrowful love may never be told;
> Cover it up with a lonely tune.
> He who could bend all things to His will
> Has covered the door of the infinite fold
> With the pale stars and the wandering moon.[21]

In 1913 Yeats scrapped this song and wrote the following:

> Were I but crazy for love's sake
> I know who'd measure out his length,
> I know the heads that I should break,
> For crazy men have double strength.
> I know — all's out to leave or take,

Who mocks at music mocks at love;
Were I but crazy for love's sake,
No need to pick and choose.
                    Enough!
I know the heads that I should break.

By changing Aleel's language Yeats made a realistic character out of the figure who in 1895 had, like the Hanrahan
of 1897, spoken with that 'sweet insinuating feminine
voice of the dwellers in that country of shadows and hol-
low images',[22] a voice which by 1903 Yeats had begun to
get rid of in his lyric verse.

Although there is no manuscript material available which
indicates exactly how Yeats used peasant speech as a
corrective to his own poetry, the major change of style
which begins — as has been frequently noted — in such
poems as 'The Folly of Being Comforted' and 'Adam's
Curse' from *In the Seven Woods* is marked by the very
features Yeats praised in the dialect: the naming of things
that have direct personal connotation, the use of images
taken from common experience, and the idioms of the
spoken voice; as may be seen in such lines as 'I have not a
crumb of comfort, not a grain' or '. . . he kneaded in the
dough/Through the long years of youth' (*C.P.*, p.86), or
in:

I said, 'A line will take us hours maybe;
Yet if it does not seem a moment's thought,
Our stitching and unstitching has been naught.
Better go down upon your marrow-bones
And scrub a kitchen pavement, or break stones
Like an old pauper, in all kinds of weather . . .'
                    ('Adam's Curse')

That it was not merely Yeats's practice in writing for the
stage which brought about this change is confirmed by a
letter he wrote in 1913 to Lady Gregory about Ezra
Pound:

He [Pound] is full of the middle ages and helps me to
get back to the definite and concrete away from modern
abstractions. To talk over a poem with him is like getting you to put a sentence into dialect. All becomes
clear and natural.[23]

It seems that the learning process Yeats describes was a
two-way affair, for in Pound's translations from Fenellosa
there are a number of examples of Anglo-Irish dialect
syntax, particularly in the first play, *Nishikigi:*

There never was anybody heard of Mount Shinobu but
had a kind feeling for it . . .
. . . It is a flag of the night I see coming down upon me.
I wonder now, would the sea be that way, or the little
place Kefu that they say is stuck down against it?[24]

But Anglo-Irish dialect had a more pervasive effect on
Yeats than that provided by a corrective exercise; it was,
after all, the speech he had heard as a child in Sligo.
Despite the fact that, as Yeats himself said, he 'never
acquired the gift of using the dialect with any realism or
precision',[25] after 1900 — and increasingly in the later
volumes of verse — aspects of its syntax become a recognisable feature of his style.

3 FEATURES OF ANGLO-IRISH DIALECT USAGE IN YEATS'S *COLLECTED POEMS*

Nowhere in Yeats's poetry is there found as sustained a use
of dialect as in the prose and verse of Hyde, Lady Gregory
and Synge. The *Collected Poems* contain, however, a
sufficient number of the features identified by P. L. Henry
and others[26] as characteristic of Anglo-Irish dialect usage
to distinguish Yeats's style quite markedly as that of an
Irish poet. What follows here is a selection of the most
prevalent and the most striking examples.

Lexical features
Although linguistically naive in its distinctions, P. W.
Joyce's *English as we speak it in Ireland,* published in

1910, contains a useful index of Anglo-Irish idiom and vocabulary. The list is not exhaustive; nor, since it is drawn from all parts of Ireland (including Ulster) can it be used as an altogether accurate guide to Yeats's experience of dialect usage; but it does cover the period of Yeats's most active interest in 'the language of the people' and it shows that there were some hundreds of dialect words in use at that time. Those Yeats uses can be divided into two categories. First of all, there are words which are readily recognised by their spelling. Whether, like 'slieveen' (*C.P.*, p. 24), they are Gaelic words directly transposed into English, or whether they are hybrid in origin, such words are clearly not in standard English usage. Although they are nowhere very numerous, words of this kind occur most frequently in Yeats's early verse, particularly in the four early ballads whose stories were taken from existing prose accounts of one kind or another (*C.P.*, pp. 23, 24, 26, 53). There are very few examples after *The Rose* (1893): 'Lebeen-lone', 'skelping', 'bawn', and 'thraneen' (*C.P.*, pp. 125, 129, 220, 296). Secondly, there are dialect words identical in spelling to words in standard English usage which have a different meaning in Anglo-Irish. Occasionally this difference is pointed up grammatically, as in 'And the fret is on me' (*Variorum*, p. 131). In English this structure would be very unusual, whereas in Anglo-Irish 'fret' is used as a noun and means 'doom'. If there are no grammatical distinctions, Yeats sometimes helps the reader by putting a dialect word into single inverted commas, as in 'Then darkening through "dark" Raftery's "cellar" drop' (*C.P.*, p. 275). Here Yeats is consciously using a word which has a specific meaning in Anglo-Irish ('dark' means 'blind') together with one which I assume has only a local meaning (Hyde explains that Raftery's 'cellar' refers to 'a great deep pool in the river, near where the house was')[27] and we are left to discover from the context of Yeats's other writings, from his notes or from his sources what those meanings are.

There are, however, more numerous instances where Yeats, without indicating that he is doing so, uses a word which is identical in spelling and grammatical function to English usage, but which has an additional or more specific meaning in Anglo-Irish. The trouble here is of course that it is impossible to tell whether he is consciously using such words in their dialectal sense; indeed, he may not have been aware that distinctions can be made. On the other hand, he may have assumed that the word in standard usage contains the meanings he intended, meanings which are in fact exclusive to dialect usage. The contextual validity of the dialect meaning of a word strongly suggests that the poet consciously intends that meaning; even so, this cannot be asserted conclusively if the standard usage also fits the poem. For example, the line 'A living man is blind and drinks his drop' (*C.P.*, p. 266) gains additional connotation from the Anglo-Irish usage of the word 'drop'. P. W. Joyce says that it means:

> A strain of any kind 'running in the blood'. A man inclined to evil ways 'has a bad drop' in him (or 'a black drop'): a miser has 'a hard drop'. The expression carries an idea of heredity.[28]

Yeats in the very next line uses the word 'ditches' in the English, not the Anglo-Irish sense (where it means a raised wall); and, except that the Anglo-Irish meaning of the word 'drop' does enrich the poem, it is of course not open to proof whether Yeats knew this meaning of the word or that he used in this way. In the poem 'His Memories', Yeats uses the word 'shows' in a way that one could argue is consciously Anglo-Irish since its meaning in standard English, although not in any sense foreign to the context, does appear somewhat awkward (less awkward, however, in American than in English usage). When we understand that in Anglo-Irish the word carries a sense of the contemptuous, the poem gains in exactness of meaning:

We should be hidden from their eyes,
Being but holy shows,
And bodies broken like a thorn
Whereon the bleak north blows . . .   (*C.P.*, p. 251)

Words of this second type appear very rarely in the early
volumes, but several examples can be seen in Yeats's later
work, particularly in *Last Poems*. Further examples include: 'black wind' (*C.P.*, p. 90) where 'black' means 'of
evil omen, fatal, accursed'[29] in a much stronger sense than
is usually the case when it is used metaphorically in standard English; 'warty lads' (*C.P.*, p. 358) where 'warty' con-
notes sexual prowess; 'airy' (*C.P.*, p. 379) which Yeats's
note tells us means 'eerie', and which P. W. Joyce states is
a survival of the old Irish pagan belief that air demons were
the most malignant of all supernatural beings;[30] and
'destroys' (*C.P.*, p. 350) which in Anglo-Irish means
'exhausts'.[31]

Whatever their origin may be, and whether or not Yeats
was aware of their specific dialectal meaning, the function
of single words is necessarily very limited. In so far as
distinctions can be made between what is said and how it
is said, dialect words contribute more to content than to
manner precisely because a single word cannot affect the
grammar of a poem. Except where the use of a dialect
word leads Yeats, consciously or not, to adopt the idiom
and syntax in which that word is most commonly found,
vocabulary itself has very little to do with what Yeats
learned from Anglo-Irish dialect.

Syntactical features

These are much more prevalent in Yeats's poetry than the
lexical examples, and most of them occur in the volumes
published after 1900; what examples there are before this
date come from those poems which are based on the words
of a peasant, as in the original version of 'The Lamentation
of the Old Pensioner', or from poems written before 1900

which were revised later on. The most numerous syntactical features occur in the volumes from *The Wild Swans at
Coole* onwards, and like the lexical examples they are
particularly evident in *Last Poems.*

I 'That' and 'what'

Yeats's use of 'that' and 'what' most consistently marks his
later style as distinctively Anglo-Irish. MacDonald Emslie's
essay 'Gestures in Scorn of an Audience'[32] gives a percep-
tive analysis of the various effects achieved by Yeats in his
use of these words; and Richard Ellmann, in *The Identity
of Yeats,* points out that used as a demonstrative adjective
the word 'that' involves the reader 'in common awareness
of what the poet is talking about, as if the poet's world
contained only objects which were readily recognisable'.[33]
There are very many examples of this usage; these are
representative:

> That lover of a night
> Came when he would . . .   (*C.P.,* p. 293)
>
> Recall that masculine Trinity . . .   (*C.P.,* p. 328)
>
> Could that old god rise up again
> We'd drink a can or two . . .   (*C.P.,* p. 371)

P. L. Henry lists the use of 'that' as a demonstrative adjective as typical of the Anglo-Irish dialect he describes,[34] but
it is also standard English usage. The common Anglo-Irish
use of 'that' as a relative pronoun instead of 'who' is,
however, rarer in standard English. Ellmann states that for
Yeats it was 'one of the ways of patenting the emphatic,
clear-headed personality who serves as the speaker of the
poems.'[35] This occurs dozens of times in the later volumes;
here are a few examples:

> Or meddle with our give and take
> That converse bone to bone?   (*C.P.,* p. 205)
>
> All things fall and are built again,
> And those that build them again are gay.   (*C.P.,* p. 339)

To this most gallant gentleman
That is in quicklime laid.   (*C.P.,* p. 352)

The word 'what' in Yeats's poetry occurs in several
syntactical contexts, each of which P. L. Henry illustrates
as being typical of Anglo-Irish dialect. I give below some
notable examples:

(*a*) *'What' used as an interrogative adjective*
Henry gives: What Michael would he be?
                 What man did you see?[36]

Here the linguistic characteristic is that of giving definite
specification. In standard English the 'what' would be replaced by 'which' in the first example, but in the second
both adjective and noun would most most commonly be
replaced by the indefinite '*Whom* did you see?', losing the
emphasis on the noun. There are some twenty instances of
this usage in Yeats's poetry, for example:

Among what rushes will they build
By what lake's edge or pool
Delight men's eyes . . .   (*C.P.,* p. 148)

What lively lad most pleasured me
Of all that with me lay?   (*C.P.,* p. 313)

What stalked through the Post Office? What intellect,
What calculation, number, measurement, replied?
                                    (*C.P.,* p. 375)

In this final example, the emphasis given by the use of
'what' as an interrogative adjective keeps the syntax of the
main clause clear through three and a half lines of quali-
fying description:

What youthful mother, a shape upon her lap
Honey of generation had betrayed,
And that must sleep, shriek, struggle to escape
As recollection or the drug decide,

Would think her son, did she but see that shape
With sixty or more winters on its head,
A compensation for the pang of his birth,
Or the uncertainty of his setting forth.   (*C.P.*, p. 244)

There are also a few instances of the same usage in
exclamatory rather than interrogative form, and some
without either.

(*b*) *'What' used in the sense of 'that which'*
Henry gives four categories of this use in Anglo-Irish:

   (i) As pure relative pronoun: 'What he won't see she'll
       see.'
  (ii) In the quantitative (numerical) sense, meaning as
       much (many) as: 'I gave her what was in the hot-
       houses'.
 (iii) Used in precise designation where in standard
       English no designative is used: 'She's better than
       what he was'.
  (iv) Used in a differentiating connection: 'It isn't what
       he'd say, but what he'd do [that counts].'[37]

Here are a few examples of Yeats's very frequent use of
this form:

He it has found shall find therein
What none other knows . . .   (*C.P.*, p. 314)

And copied out what I could read
In that religious gloom.   (*C.P.*, p. 353)

For Death who takes what man would keep
    Leaves what man would lose.   (*C.P.*, p. 383)

These three examples correspond to Henry's categories (i),
(ii) and (iv) respectively. Under category (ii) Henry also
lists the use of 'whatever'; in Yeats we have:

Whatever stands in field or flood,
Bird, beast, fish or man . . .   (*C.P.*, p. 305)

> Whatever's written in what poets name
> The book of the people; whatever most can bless
> The mind of man or elevate a rhyme...
>
> (*C.P.*, p. 276)

— among a few other examples where 'whatever' means 'all that which', further emphasising the syntactical ellipsis which is the main feature of this usage.

Yeats's use of the word 'what' is an important structural element in his rhetoric; its increasing incidence in the later volumes of poetry is a mark of what may be called his 'bardic' style, where the voice and techniques of the ballad poet are used as a vehicle — sometimes perhaps instrusively or histrionically — for personal subject matter.

(c) 'What' used with 'but'

There are some fifteen examples in the *Collected Poems* of this structure which P. L. Henry describes as making an emphatic statement by means of the interrogative form:[38]

> What need you, being come to sense,
> But fumble in a greasy till...?   (*C.P.*, p. 120)

> What's water but the generated soul?   (*C.P.*, p. 275)

> What theme had Homer but original sin?   (*C.P.*, p. 285)

The first example here, taken from 'September 1913', is given by Ellmann as an illustration of Yeats not writing in a common syntax but in an extremely stylised speech;[39] Henry's text clearly shows, however, that this usage is not at all 'long out of fashion' as Ellmann claims. Yeats of course sometimes enriches that structure by clauşal or phrasal qualifications or by the use of a complex word like 'generated', but its basic pattern is a common feature of Anglo-Irish dialect syntax.

II Co-ordinative use of 'and'

P. L. Henry's text gives: 'You put your nose in an' us churning.'

— You appeared while we were churning.
'You hate to go anywhere an' it raining' — . . . when it is
    raining.⁴⁰

Yeats has:

You ask what I have found, and far and wide I go:
Nothing but Cromwell's house and Cromwell's
        murderous crew.
                                        (*C.P.*, p. 350)

And there I found an old man, and though I prayed all
        day
And that old man beside me, nothing would he say . . .
                                        (*C.P.*, p. 360)

A king had some beautiful cousins,
But where are they gone?
Battered to death in a cellar,
And he stuck to his throne.   (*C.P.*, p. 390)

There are a few examples of this structure with the 'and'
omitted, as in:

Or anything else but a rhymer
Without a thing in his head
But rhymes for a beautiful lady,
He rhyming alone in his bed.   (*C.P.*, p. 326)

That most of the ten examples of this usage come from the
last two volumes of poetry gives evidence that as Yeats
turned to the ballad form at the end of his career he relied
more heavily than ever before — apart from his consistent
use of it in several of his plays — on Anglo-Irish syntax.

III Concrete specification

P. L. Henry gives examples of the Anglo-Irish dialect usage
of the definite article, the indefinite article and the demonstrative adjective, which he argues illustrates a mode of
specification more concrete and immediate than is normally found in standard English.⁴¹ Although Yeats very

rarely uses the definite article in similar ways to Henry's examples — Yeats has 'O love is the crooked thing' (*C.P.*, p. 110) which parallels Henry's 'He has never the good word to say' — he does frequently use the indefinite article to specify by a single detail, usually qualified adjectivally. Henry gives: 'Not a man nor a woman of them would know' — None of them would know.[42]

An early example in Yeats occurs in *In the Seven Woods* (1903): 'There's no man may look upon her, no man' (*C.P.*, p. 85). The following lines are taken from a poem in *The Rose* (1893), but they are from the extensive revisions of 1925:

> That country where a man can be so crossed;
> Can be so battered, badgered and destroyed
> That he's a loveless man . . .   (*C.P.*, p. 51)

In another revision we have:

> There's not a woman turns her face
> Upon a broken tree . . .   (*C.P.*, p. 52)

In the next example the specifying of 'no man' more readily allows the syntactical emphasis which follows 'but' than would be possible with the use of 'no one': 'And there's no man but cocks his ear' (*C.P.*, p. 133). Qualified specification occurs often in the later volumes of poetry, as in:

> A living man is blind and drinks his drop   (*C.P.*, p. 266)

> Did I become a Christian man . . .   (*C.P.*, p. 285)

> And a proud man's a lovely man   (*C.P.*, p. 356)

> A statesman is an easy man   (*C.P.*, p. 365)

The example given earlier from Henry's text of the dialect habit of specifying concretely — 'Bridget lost the breath' — can be compared with Yeats's:

> . . . a melancholy man
> Who had ended where his breath began.   (*C.P.,* p. 176)

> Lay in the coffin, stopped his breath and died.
>   (*C.P.,* p. 374)

But apart from such close parallels to Henry's examples, the strength of Yeats's style as it developed after 1900 owes a great deal to his increasing use of the concrete and particular. Perhaps the starkest instance of his use of 'the common idiom' is:

> Saint Joseph thought the world would melt
> But liked the way his finger smelt.   (*C.P.,* p. 383)

But sometimes the particularisation comes through a complex word, as in:

> I offer to love's play
> My dark declivities.   (*C.P.,* p. 312)

IV Occasional parallels

There are a number of examples of Yeats's usage that correspond, with varying exactness, to that common in Anglo-Irish dialect. Henry notes that the Anglo-Irish inversion of normal English word order, which is governed by opening a sentence with 'it's' or a variant (whose source lies in Gaelic), is a device for presenting the speaker's thought as directly as possible, and that the possibility of emphasis is latent in all the examples he gives,[43] as in:

> ' 'Twas a bullock we had.'
> 'It's at home she should be.'

Although Yeats never begins a sentence with 'it's' in this manner, he does occasionally use the same kind of inversion for exactly the same purpose of stressing what is most important, as in:

> 'A young man in the dark am I,
> But a wild old man in the light . . .'   (*C.P.,* p. 357)

Yeats was using this kind of inversion as early as 'The Lake Isle of Innisfree':

> ... a small cabin build there ...
> Nine bean rows will I have there ...   (*C.P.,* p. 44)

The closeness of Yeats's rhythms in this poem to Ferguson's translation 'The Fair Hills of Ireland' is in part due to the same feature:

> A plenteous place is Ireland for hospitable cheer ...
> Large and profitable are the stocks upon the ground ...

The inversion Yeats regretted having left in 'Innisfree' was solely in the placing of the adjective in 'pavements grey'; to have altered the inversion of subject and predicate in the first stanza would have meant the loss of the poem's distinctive rhythm. Many of the translators from the Gaelic use the feature Henry describes, most notably Douglas Hyde.

Another kind of inversion occurs in dialect usage in a structure which Henry, referring to Jesperson, defines as being controlled by the use of *empty* 'there', where this word precedes the verb, which in turn precedes the subject. He notes that this usage is reminiscent of Gaelic word order, and that its function is of emphasis on the actuality of the event described.[44] One example from Yeats vividly illustrates the latter comment:

> ... thereupon
> There lurches past, his great eyes without thought
> Under the shadow of stupid pale-straw locks,
> That insolent fiend Robert Artisson ...   (*C.P.,* p. 237)

The last example of minor parallels in structure has to do with tense sequence. In a long section on 'Tense', P. L. Henry notes that 'the traditional rhetorical strain in the Anglo-Irish speaker can be traced in his preference for tenses which impress and persuade'. Being primarily concerned with giving emphasis and the sense of actuality, he will often combine past and future in the same sentence. In one example given by Henry, the past indicative is used for an eventuality in future time; and in the same sentence a future is used for a conditional: 'If they came that they were in the way even, I'll not touch them'.

Henry explains: 'The key to this usage of the future for conditional is that the content of the *if*-clause is visualised as being actual and the future is chosen to express definiteness, certainty, assurance. The certainty conveyed by the future here balances the sense of actuality expressed by the past.'[45] The following quotations from Yeats show a tense sequence quite unfamiliar to standard English usage:

> . . . and if we turn about
> The bare chimney is gone black out.   (*C.P.*, p. 151)

> So arrogantly pure, a child might think
> It can be murdered with a spot of ink.   (*C.P.*, p. 276)

> . . . A voice cried, 'The Fenians a long time are dead'.
>   (*C.P.*, p. 443)

The last example is a clear case of the Anglo-Irish 'expanded present', but neither of the other two has a precise equivalent in P. L. Henry's text. Their purpose and effect, however, is exactly as in the examples given by Henry: they transfer the sense from the indefinite to the definite and actual.

Although for the most part Yeats's usage in the examples given in this chapter is not exclusively that of the Anglo-Irish dialect described by Professor Henry, the frequent similarity of syntax argues strongly for the influence of native speech patterns in his verse. Yeats said of Synge's use of dialect that 'it gave him imaginative richness and yet left to him the sting and tang of reality';[45] and although he admitted he could never use it as Synge did, Anglo-Irish speech not only served Yeats as a model for his most important change of style, it also marked that style in an increasing measure throughout his subsequent development.

V Ballad Rhetoric

1 THE POLITICAL BALLADS

Writing to Katharine Tynan in 1906, Yeats accused contemporary Irish poets of being 'vague, self-conscious, literary; the reverse of the young poets of our young days who were not literary at all — I remember getting into trouble for calling them electioneering rhymers.'[1] In complete contrast to his emphasis only a few years earlier on the need to create an 'aristocratic, esoteric Irish literature', his plan for improving these contemporary poets was to have them write songs to be sung between the acts at the Abbey Theatre. The implication is plain: a song, because it must communicate directly to a listening, not a reading audience, cannot be 'literary' in the pejorative sense in which Yeats now used that word; and in adapting traditional songs for his plays he was acting on his own advice. Yeats had escaped from a vague literary style by drawing upon the language of his native folk tradition, but when he began writing political ballads he used the concreteness and rhetorical energy he had learned from dialect syntax to invoke that other, very different tradition of Young Ireland 'electioneering' verse which in 1895 he had rejected as spurious.

In 'September 1913', one of the group of poems written around the public theme of the Lane Controversy, Yeats scornfully addresses a mass audience and generates considerable ironic force by confronting them with their former idealism as it was expressed in the popular verse of Thomas Davis and his followers in the Young Ireland movement. The poem opens with a bitter attack on contemporary Ireland where both religion and materialism mark the same narrowness of spirit:

> What need you, being come to sense,
> But fumble in a greasy till
> And add the halfpence to the pence
> And prayer to shivering prayer, until
> You have dried the marrow from the bone?
> For men were born to pray and save:
> Romantic Ireland's dead and gone,
> It's with O'Leary in the grave.

Throughout the poem the refrain, with a slight but very effective change in the last stanza, counterpoints the irony in its bald, idiomatic statement of what has been lost. The third stanza draws on the bastardised form of the ballad found in *The Spirit of the Nation* in such trite stanzas as:

> The wild geese — the wild geese — 'tis long since they
>   flew
> O'er the billowy ocean's bright bosom of blue,
> For the foot of the false-hearted stranger had curst
> The shores on whose fond breast they'd settled at first.

(A note explains that recruits of the Irish Brigade were taken to France and entered on the ships' books as 'Wild Geese'.)

Or as these equally atrocious lines from Davis's 'The Green Above the Red':

> Sure 'twas for this Lord Edward died, and Wolfe Tone
>   sunk serene —
> Because they could not bear to leave the Red above the
>   Green.
> And 'twas for this that Owen fought, and Sarsfield
>   nobly bled —
> Because their eyes were hot to see the Green above the
>   Red.

Yeats's reference to Davis's poem is clear:

> Was it for this the wild geese spread
> The grey wing on every tide;
> For this that all that blood was shed,
> For this Edward Fitzgerald died,
> And Robert Emmet and Wolfe Tone,
> All that delirium of the brave?
> Romantic Ireland's dead and gone,
> It's with O'Leary in the grave.

Within this stanza's powerful exhortation the ironic tone of the poem is held in the line: 'All that delirium of the brave?', where Yeats uses a word which both defines the changed attitude of his audience to heroism and at the same time accuses them of a poverty of imagination which is made explicit in the final stanza.

Whereas only two of the four stanzas of 'September 1913' structurally owe their emphasis to the rhetorical question, 'Sixteen Dead Men' relies almost entirely on this device which is based upon the confident assumption that the subject matter is public knowledge. The argument is clear: the shooting of the leaders of the Easter Rising has made the Irish cause into an issue that can no longer be negotiated in terms of reason:

> You say that we should still the land
> Till Germany's overcome;
> But who is there to argue that
> Now Pearse is deaf and dumb?
> And is their logic to outweigh
> MacDonagh's bony thumb?

And the third stanza emphasises the community of spirit of the sixteen dead men with former Irish political heroes. Here again we have the naming of names of the Young Irelanders, but whereas those poets had carried such balladic evocation in a second-hand style, full of clichés and crude, generalised description, Yeats intensifies the rhetorical impact by employing common idioms in a starker and more specific sense than their standard usage. The poem combines Young Ireland balladry with a descriptive realism which is much more truly native to Irish literature, but it is the former which sets the oratorical tone.

'The Rose Tree' is the closest of this group of poems to the popular style as we know it in the Anglo-Scots tradition. The repetition of the names Pearse and Connolly, designed as a refrain in each stanza, announces that these men are taken as established ballad characters. There is none of the rhetorical persuasion which in 'September 1913' and 'Sixteen Dead Men' calls upon the past as a measure of what public feeling should be or is, and makes an identification with a former political passion. 'The Rose Tree' is entirely impersonal and objective; and by dialogue alone it deals dramatically with a single event. The poem differs from the general characteristics of the Anglo-Scots ballad first in giving the reasons for the action rather than describing what happened, and secondly in the allusiveness of its language. Here are its first and third stanzas:

> 'O WORDS are lightly spoken,'
> Said Pearse to Connolly,
> 'Maybe a breath of politic words
> Has withered our Rose Tree;
> Or maybe but a wind that blows
> Across the bitter sea.'
>
> 'But where can we draw water',
> Said Pearse to Connolly,
> 'When all the wells are parched away?
> O plain as plain can be
> There's nothing but our own red blood
> Can make a right Rose Tree.'

In combining nationalism and religious consciousness, the poem draws upon two of the most central of Irish subjects.

The Rose symbol which Yeats had used in his esoteric poetry in the 1890s — and which, as he later admitted, had become unintelligible to the popular audience he was trying to reach — now becomes an unequivocal political emblem. Behind it lie two Irish traditions: that of the street ballad theme of a 'Liberty Tree' which is nourished, as the song has it, by 'The pure blood of Ireland's Martyrs';[2] and that of the Gaelic *aisling* poem, where Ireland is represented as a beautiful woman whose protection calls for ultimate sacrifice. In the first stanza Yeats uses the common idiomatic reference to England, 'across the water', in alluding to the stultifying influence of English rule as '. . . a wind that blows/Across the bitter sea'. The second stanza employs the simple, unambiguous symbol of watering the Rose Tree that is Ireland, and makes sure of its popular appeal by using the sentimental cliché — common property of Young Ireland verse and of music hall song — in which green signifies rebirth, freedom and beauty. But the implicit religious identification in time (the Rising occurred on Easter Monday) and symbol of the Irish leaders' self-sacrifice suddenly transforms the poem's meaning. A comparison with his early attempts to evoke religious feeling in the ballads about Moll Magee and Father Gilligan shows that by 1920 Yeats had learned that if a popular balladry is to be made out of events, those events must be important, public and contemporary; that, in essence, the poet's subject-matter is no different from the street balladeer's. In this poem he was at last able to tap those vast forces of feeling, political and religious, which he had always seen as distinctively Irish but which in the 1890s he had wanted to channel into what he considered to be more discriminating subjects and responses.

2 THE PERSONAL POEM

A clue to the way Yeats intended 'The Rose Tree' to be read aloud is given by V.C. Clinton-Baddeley's report that his instructions were to speak the refrain line, 'Said Pearse

to Connolly', with an heraldic swing.[4] The subject in
Yeats's political ballads is news for the public ear, whereas
in his personal poetry of this period the subject is for the
private ear alone. There is no oratorical tone; no balladic
shorthand, and no appeal through questions that imply
their own answers. Nothing is preconceived. In 'Cold
Heaven', the poet is finding out what his thoughts and
feelings really are: a soliloquy of personal investigation;
and the question he asks at the end of the poem is
primarily addressed to himself, and is unanswerable:

> . . . Ah! when the ghost begins to quicken,
> Confusion of the death-bed over, is it sent
> Out naked on the roads, as the books say, and stricken
> By the injustice of the skies for punishment?

One of the best examples of this sort of poem is seen in
'Under Saturn':

> Do not because this day I have grown saturnine
> Imagine that lost love, inseparable from my thought
> Because I have no other youth, can make me pine;
> For how should I forget the wisdom that you brought,
> The comfort that you made? Although my wits have
>   gone
> On a fantastic ride, my horse's flanks are spurred
> By childish memories of an old cross Pollexfen,
> And of a Middleton, whose name you never heard,
> And of a red-haired Yeats whose looks, although he died
> Before my time, seem like a vivid memory.
> You heard that labouring man who had served my
>   people. He said
> Upon the open road, near to the Sligo quay —
> No, no, not said, but cried it out — 'You have come
>   again,
> And surely after twenty years it was time to come.'
> I am thinking of a child's vow sworn in vain
> Never to leave that valley his fathers called their home.

The poem's syntactical energy depends wholly on clausal qualifications which carry the argument so successfully that the rhyme is barely noticeable. It is a particularly interesting example of Yeats's personal voice because although it uses proper names and one place name, it is entirely without rhetorical appeal; the poem explicitly states that they are not tokens for anything but a private memory, one that the poet does not try to elevate to a public status. There is no exhortation, no banner waved in ballad shorthand: the emphasis in the words of the 'labouring man', which is a statement in the form of a question, serves merely to expose dramatically the poem's personal theme. Yeats has created feeling by explaining his thought.

'Easter 1916', which is perhaps Yeats's most famous poem on a public theme, gets its richness of texture from the combination of both styles, ballad and personal. It opens with a careful explanation of how the poet's own attitude to Ireland has been changed by the heroism of particular people:

> I have met them at close of day
> Coming with vivid faces
> From counter or desk among grey
> Eighteenth century houses.
> I have passed with a nod of the head
> Or polite meaningless words . . .
> Being certain that they and I
> But lived where motley is worn:
> All changed, changed utterly:
> A terrible beauty is born.

The poem then explores a complex reaction first to what dangers are inherent in martyrdom to a cause, and secondly to the validity of its purpose. But the first aspect is not solely concerned with the subject of the poem: it has obvious biographical resonances in Yeats's feelings about Maud Gonne,[4] and its lyrical description is a means of defining his own personal response to experience which is summarised in the opening lines of the next stanza:

> Too long a sacrifice
> Can make a stone of the heart.

The sensitive equivocation of feeling about the death of the leaders of the Easter Rising which follows is carried through questions that are not rhetorical in any sense:

> What is it but nightfall?
> No, no, not night but death;
> Was it needless death after all?
> For England may keep faith
> For all that is done and said.

Yet in the next line the poem again changes tone and mood. The ambivalence of Yeats's personal response to the meaning of the political sacrifice is cast away in the recognition that

> We know their dream; enough
> To know they dreamed and are dead;
> And what if excess of love
> Bewildered them till they died?

Faced with the fact of what has happened, it makes no difference what opinions or emotions one may privately entertain; and it is at this point that the balladic note takes over:

> I write it out in a verse —
> MacDonagh and MacBride
> And Connolly and Pearse
> Now and in time to be,
> Wherever green is worn,
> Are changed, changed utterly:
> A terrible beauty is born.

Yeats here speaks the names of the Irish heroes in a deliberate litany from the Young Ireland text,[5] including — with no sense of incongruity — a line which echoes the sentimental tradition of the song 'The Wearin' of the Green'. 'Easter 1916' ends in an identification with a popular mode and so carries with it a history of national feeling. The ballad style signals Yeats's tribute to a fact that needs no explaining: the token names and the manner in which they are named strike to the heart of Irish national consciousness.

3 THE VOICE OF THE BARD

Ezra Pound quotes Yeats as saying:

> I have spent the whole of my life trying to get rid of rhetoric. I have got rid of one kind of rhetoric and have merely set up another.[6]

Pound vaguely dates this statement as being made 'between 1912-1918', but it can be very appropriately applied to what was happening some ten years later. The changes Yeats made in 'The Lamentation of the Old Pensioner' in 1925 are indicative of changes occurring in his style at that time. Yeats makes a more powerful poem out of the two stanzas which he first printed as 'an almost verbatim record of words by an old Irishman', but in dramatising the old man's predicament in 1925 he comes perilously close to the histrionic. The danger lies in the pensioner's defiance of Time carrying a tone of exaggerated self-awareness and self-importance:

> I spit into the face of Time
> That has transfigured me.

It is just such a tone which begins to enter Yeats's personal poetry, and here it is less innocuous because there is no persona masking the self-dramatisation. The title poem of *The Tower,* despite its many fine qualities, is disturbing because of the frequent posturing of the speaker, the insistent 'I' of the poem. At one point the audience (whom Yeats thinks of as listening rather than reading) is sup-

posed so completely under the speaker's spell as to be able
to put up with the third line here:

> Hanrahan rose in frenzy there
> And followed those baying creatures towards —
>
> O towards I have forgotten what — enough!

And the third section of the poem is repeatedly declamatory:

> It is time that I wrote my will;
> I choose upstanding men . . .
>   . . . I declare
> They shall inherit my pride . . .
> And I declare my faith:
> I mock Plotinus' thought
> And cry in Plato's teeth . . .

The tone of the rest of the poem is controlled by this
testamentary syntax; but it is not at all fortuitous that we
hear the rhythms of:

> I write it out in a verse —
> MacDonagh and MacBride
> And Connolly and Pearse . . .

At this point in 'Easter 1916' the 'I' serves merely to intro-
duce a balladic note which is perfectly appropriate to the
subject. When Yeats alluded to the Young Ireland tradition
in his political ballads the public events celebrated by
those ballads were the source of their passion and entirely
validated their rhetorical energy; his personal voice, however, becomes the more strident exactly as his imagination
depends increasingly upon the events in his own life being
built into a private mythology. When Yeats makes ballad
material out of his own framework of references — his
situation in Ireland, his home, friends and family — the
spoken word is at times in danger of becoming the instru-
ment of a rhetorical persuasion that is purely self-
regarding. It can lead to such flatness as:

Having inherited a vigorous mind
From my old fathers, I must nourish dreams
And leave a woman and a man behind
As vigorous of mind . . .

('My Descendants')

Or to the bombast of:

I declare that this tower is my symbol; I declare
This winding, gyring, spiring treadmill of a stair is my
    ancestral stair;
That Goldsmith and the Dean, Berkeley and Burke have
    travelled there.

('Blood and the Moon')

The very images he uses become a kind of shorthand and
assume the token connotation of a name in a ballad:

An ancient bridge, and a more ancient tower,
A farmhouse that is sheltered by its wall,
An acre of stony ground,
Where the symbolic rose can break in flower,
Old ragged elms, old thorns innumerable . . .

('My House')

Only rarely do we hear the rhythms of Yeats's earlier personal voice, formed as they are in such poems as 'The Cold
Heaven', 'Under Saturn' and 'A Prayer for My Daughter'
by a syntax whose statements are constantly qualified by
parenthetic clauses which give the sense of the poet enquir-
ing into the nature of his feeling. Those rhythms are there
in 'The New Faces':

If you, that have grown old, were the first dead,
Neither catalpa tree nor scented lime
Should hear my living feet . . .

But this poem was written in 1912 and not published until
1928. By the 1920s the devices of Yeats's political ballads
are being used in his lyric verse. The reader may feel he is

being tricked into an intimacy with the poet's experience
when Yeats invokes the names of his friends:

> There Hyde before he had beaten into prose
> That noble blade the Muses buckled on,
> There one that ruffled in a manly pose
> For all his timid heart, there that slow man,
> That meditative man, John Synge, and those
> Impetuous men, Shawe-Taylor and Hugh Lane . . .

Later, in 'The Municipal Gallery Revisited', Yeats speaks
of the portraits he describes as: '. . . that tale/As though
some ballad-singer had sung it all'. Although there are
touches· of self-dramatisation in both poems, their rhetoric
does have a wider context. Yeats said of 'The Municipal
Gallery Revisited' that it was 'a poem about the Ireland we
have all served, and the movement of which I have been a
part'; an Ireland which was 'a great pictured song'.[7]

    In *The Tower* Yeats frequently adopts an oratorical
tone:

> What if those things the greatest of mankind
> Consider most to magnify, or to bless,
> But take our greatness with our bitterness?
>
> > ('Ancestral Houses')
>
> And what if my descendants lose the flower
> Through natural declension of the soul . . .?
>
> > ('My Descendants')
>
> What matter that no cannon has been turned
> Into a ploughshare?
>
> > ('Nineteen Hundred and Nineteen')

But he does not always pose a question that assumes its
own answer. In 'A Dialogue of Self and Soul', from the
next volume, the lines:

> A living man is blind and drinks his drop,
> What matter if the ditches are impure
> What matter if I live it all once more . . .?

are followed by a description of the toil, ignominy and distress of growing up; then by a rhetorical question which vividly defines its meaning in a syntax so organic to thought that this section of the stanza cannot be read aloud adequately except in one breath:

> How in the name of Heaven can he escape
> That defiling and disfigured shape
> The mirror of malicious eyes
> Casts upon his eyes until at last
> He thinks that shape must be his shape?

The poem ends on assertive answers to the questions asked:

> I am content to live it all again
> And yet again . . .
>
> When such as I cast out remorse
> So great a sweetness flows into the breast . . .

— though even here it may appear to some readers as an embarrassing parading of the self.

VI Passionate Syntax

1 THE SONG SEQUENCES IN *THE TOWER* AND *THE WINDING STAIR*

Although 'A Man Young and Old' is for the most part only slightly veiled autobiography — 'I have written', Yeats said, 'the wild regrets for youth and love of an old man'[1] — there is no sense of the strident or histrionic because in these songs the function of the syntax, like that of the intimate personal poem, is to reveal the nature of experience through the sequence of thought that expresses it. Writing to H.J.C. Grierson in 1926, Yeats explained what changes were occurring in his style:

> I am particularly indebted to you for your essay on Byron. My own verse has more and more adopted . . . the syntax and vocabulary of common personal speech. . . . The over childish or over pretty element in some good Wordsworth and in much poetry up to our date comes from the lack of natural momentum in the syntax. This momentum underlies almost every Elizabethan and Jacobean lyric and is far more important than simplicity of vocabulary. If Wordsworth had found it he could have carried any amount of elaborate English.[2]

In the essay Yeats refers to,[3] Grierson writes of the importance of Byron's influence on modern poetry. He argues that the line of tradition from Keats through Tennyson to Rossetti, Morris and Swinburne ended in a too conscious artistry, in a concern with 'the beauty of things somewhat remote from life'; Byron, on the other hand — and, within the limits of his subject, Kipling too — kept alive the tradi-

tion of poetry that deals with actual experience in a tone
at once passionate and personal, the best examples of
which are found in Jonson, Donne and Burns. The word
'momentum' is Grierson's, and he clarifies what he means
by it in reference to the work of these poets: it is not the
same thing as 'speed', for Swinburne has Byron's speed; it
has to do with an energy of feeling centred on subjects of
common experience so that the experience itself has pre-
eminence in the poem, not the idealising of it, nor the
sensuous description of it, nor the philosophising about it.
Grierson's statements in 1925 echo Yeats's ideas twenty
years earlier on the need for a language that deals directly
with the life of 'the whole man', and Yeats had already
shown that he understood it was a matter of syntax not
merely of vocabulary. In 1916 he wrote in a manuscript
book: 'If a poem talks . . . we have the passionate syntax,
the impression of the man who speaks, the active man, no
abstract poet';[4] and in an interview with the *Irish Times*
when he was awarded the Nobel Prize in 1923, he declared
that the aim of all his work had been to perfect the syntax
of passionate speech. The report of the interview continues:

> One ought to be able to declaim a lyric, he said, in a
> market square so that the people who heard it hardly
> would recognise that they were not listening to prose.
> Wordsworth had broken new ground by his discovery of
> the vocabulary of such speech . . . he [Yeats] had
> striven to find its syntax.[5]

In the songs of 'A Man Young and Old' Yeats uses a syntax
which moves through several lines, often through a complete stanza, within the syllabic form of the fourteener,
traditionally the vehicle of simple narrative:

> Like the moon her kindness is,
> If kindness I may call
> What has no comprehension in't,
> But is the same for all

> As though my sorrow were a scene
> Upon a painted wall.   ('Human Dignity')

There are three strong rhymes here, but the first two are immediately followed by a clausal qualification which carries the exploration of feeling forward as if it were just a statement in prose. A comparison with a stanza of an Anglo-Scots ballad illustrates how Yeats's syntax breaks through the rhythms of the traditional form:

> There lived a wife at Usher's well,
>   And a wealthy wife was she;
> She had three stout and stalwart sons.
>   And sent them o'er the sea.

Yeats's 'First Love' describes a series of actions, but they do not merely relate events:

> Though nurtured like the sailing moon
> In beauty's murderous brood,
> She walked awhile and blushed awhile
> And on my pathway stood
> Until I thought her body bore
> A heart of flesh and blood.
>
> But since I laid a hand thereon
> And found a heart of stone
> I have attempted many things
> And not a thing is done,
> For every hand is lunatic
> That travels on the moon.
>
> She smiled and that transfigured me
> And left me but a lout,
> Maundering here and maundering there,
> Emptier of thought
> Than the heavenly circuit of its stars
> When the moon sails out.

These are actions which embody feeling. Each stanza is a

complete sentence whose 'natural momentum' is entirely controlled by the poet's response to his experience. Even when Yeats simply relies on the conjunction 'and' for this fluid movement, as in the second stanza of 'The Death of the Hare', the syntax relevantly articulates the consecutive process in the speaker's recognition that the image used has an extended and more poignant meaning:

> Then suddenly my heart is wrung
> By her distracted air
> And I remember wildness lost
> And after, swept from there,
> Am set down standing in the wood
> At the death of the hare.

By 1929 the concept of 'momentum' had become so important to Yeats that he saw it as a ruling feature of his style. In an unpublished letter to Lady Gregory he said: 'When I am writing verse I must not break the momentum for if I do I lose the poem.'[6]

Several of the lyrics from 'A Woman Young and Old' (written before the publication of *The Tower* but left out of that volume) have the same syntactical structure as those of the earlier sequence:

> She hears me strike the board and say
> That she is under ban
> Of all good men and women,
> Being mentioned with a man
> That has the worst of all bad names;
> And thereupon replies
> That his hair is beautiful,
> Cold as the March wind his eyes.
>
> ('Father and Child')

To enhance the sense of the spoken voice in these poems Yeats occasionally uses rhetorical features of Anglo-Irish speech such as 'that' as relative pronoun or demonstrative adjective, and 'what' as interrogative adjective:

> . . . But stretch that body for a while
> And lay down that head
> Till I have told the sages
> Where man is comforted.   ('Consolation')

> What lively lad most pleasured me
> Of all that with me lay?
> I answer that I gave my soul
> And loved in misery,
> But had great pleasure with a lad
> That I loved bodily.   ('A Last Confession')

This usage becomes much more marked in *Words For Music Perhaps;* and because it suggests that the peasant spokesman is talking about what is familiar both to him and to his audience, it enables Yeats to include, without incongruity, a sophisticated vocabulary and classical or philosophical allusion:

> I care not what the sailors say:
> All those dreadful thunder-stones,
> All that storm that blots the day
> Can but show that Heaven yawns:
> Great Europa played the fool
> That changed a lover for a bull.
> *Fol de rol, fol de rol.*   ('Crazy Jane Reproved')

> Sang old Tom the lunatic
> That sleeps under the canopy:
> 'What change has put my thoughts astray
> And eyes that had so keen a sight?
> What has turned to smoking wick
> Nature's pure unchanging light?'
>   ('Tom the Lunatic')

Classical allusion is in any case not out of place in the tradition of Irish folk poetry as it came down in translation, even if such collections as Walsh's *Irish Popular Songs* and Hyde's *Songs Ascribed to Raftery* (1903) indicate that the allusion which the professional Gaelic poet was trained to employ in long, elaborate elegies has deteriorated to mere name-dropping in the hands of the peasant songwriter.

Yeats explained that the original title he gave this sequence, 'Twelve Poems for Music', meant 'no[t] so much as they may be sung as that I may define their kind of emotion to myself. I want them to be all emotional and all impersonal'.[7] And it is the Anglo-Scots ballad form, not just the adoption of a persona, which works towards this end. For the sake of emphasis the metre of the fourteener is sometimes completely broken:

> 'Love is all
> Unsatisfied
> That cannot take the whole
> Body and soul';
> *And that is what Jane said.*
>
> ('Crazy Jane on the Day of Judgment')

But by incorporating ballad characteristics of dialogue and/or refrain in so many of these poems Yeats objectifies his own feelings and at the same time makes it seem as if they come out of a popular tradition.

The evocative power of Yeats's style in the three song sequences has a direct link with Irish tradition since it comes from the naming of the concrete and specific. Verb force in many of these poems is minimal; most frequently it is the substantial strength of the syntax which conveys their emphasis and impact:

> The Bishop has a skin, God knows,
> Wrinkled like the foot of a goose,
> *(All find safety in the tomb.)*
> Nor can he hide in holy black
> The heron's hunch upon his back,
> But a birch-tree stood my Jack:
> *The solid man and the coxcomb.*
>
> ('Crazy Jane and the Bishop')

This economy of expression, a reduction to essentials, is first seen in Yeats's early 'Irish' poems:

> I had a chair at every hearth,
> When no one turned to see
> With 'Look at that old fellow there;
> And who may he be?'
> And therefore do I wander on,
> And the fret is on me.

It is there too in the Connacht songs translated by Douglas Hyde, in the folk songs Yeats used for his plays, and in many other translations from the Gaelic. Such a technique is not of course uniquely Irish; but since Yeats turned to his native tradition at the most important change in his poetic theory, and since there is evidence of his continued recourse to aspects of that tradition in the development of his style, the Irish heritage in these songs is clearly pre-eminent.

The main difference between Yeats's early 'Irish' poems, his sources in Hyde and in other translations from the Gaelic, and the late songs is that in the latter Yeats uses the concrete to explore the abstract. In 1906 it was plain that between the two ways he defined as open to literature, the abstract vision of a Shelley or the earthiness of a Villon, Yeats had preferred the latter — though he had warned that it was better to be a Shelley than a bad Robert Burns;[8] and in 1909 Yeats had approved of Synge's identical distinction between 'exalted verse' and 'vital verse'. Vital verse for Synge meant that which dealt with details of ordinary personal life which have, he said, 'strong roots among the clay and worms'.[9] But by 1914 Yeats was not so sure about these distinctions. In a letter to his father he wrote:

> What you say is true about abstract ideas. They are one's curse and one has sometimes to work for months before they are eliminated, or till the map has become a

country. Yet in some curious way, they are connected
with poetry or rather with passion, one half its life and
yet its enemy.[10]

In his song sequences, as in some of the ballads in *Last
Poems,* Yeats makes the map into a country by naming the
particular, intimate detail. In 'Crazy Jane Talks with the
Bishop', for example, Yeats is concerned with the inter-
dependence of body and spirit. In a manner which echoes
the early Irish poet's description of 'The Old Woman of
Beare'[11] — a figure who in 1893 had interested Yeats only
because of her magical attributes, her 'faery life'[12] — the
Bishop evokes the sense of physical debility by talking of
flat and fallen breasts and veins that must soon be dry; he
praises the life of the spirit in the biblical allusion,
'heavenly mansion', and for him the life of the body is a
'foul sty'. Crazy Jane's assertion that the spirit cannot
exist without the body is expressed within the momentum
of logical argument in the last two stanzas; her reply relies
on the same rhetorical emphasis on the specific, but its
meaning has powerful metaphoric force:

> But Love has pitched his mansion in
> The place of excrement;
> For nothing can be sole or whole
> That has not been rent.

Similarly, in 'A Last Confession', Yeats uses a forthright
description of physical love as an image for union of the
spirit:

> I gave what other women gave
> That stepped out of their clothes,
> But when this soul, its body off,
> Naked to naked goes,
> He it has found shall find therein
> What none other knows ...

Giving a clear example in its penultimate line of the concrete specification found in Anglo-Irish dialect, the last stanza is linked with the Swedenborg conception that the intercourse of angels is an incandescence:

> And give his own and take his own
> And rule in his own right;
> And though it loved in misery
> Close and cling so tight,
> There's not a bird of day that dare
> Extinguish that delight.

But the poem's abstract theme is plainly built upon common experience.

In 'A General Introduction for my Work' Yeats talks about the function of form in transmuting life into art:

> ... all that is personal soon rots; it must be packed in ice or salt. ... If I wrote of personal love or sorrow in free verse, or in any rhythm that left it unchanged, amid all its accidence, I would be full of self-contempt because of my egotism and indiscretion, and foresee the boredom of my reader. I must choose a traditional stanza, even what I alter must seem traditional.[13]

The traditional form of ballad and song provided the objectivity within which Yeats could express the self; 'those simple forms', he said, 'that like a masquer's mask protect us with their anonymity'.[14] In particular, he argues that the rhythms of the folk-singers must not be lost:

> If I repeat the first line of *Paradise Lost* so as to emphasise its five feet I am among the folk singers — 'Of mán's first dísobédience ánd the frúit', but speak it as I should I cross it with another emphasis, that of passionate prose — 'Of mán's fírst disobédience and the frúit' . . . the folk song is still there, but a ghostly voice, an unvariable possibility, an unconscious norm. What moves me and my hearer is a vivid speech that has no laws except that it must not exorcise the ghostly voice. I am awake and asleep, at my

moment of revelation, self-possessed in self-surrender; there is no rhyme, no echo of the beaten drum, the dancing foot, that would overset my balance.[15]

By the emphasis of passionate prose Yeats means the rhythms of the spoken voice, the subjective self. Thirty years earlier he had called 'personality, the breath of men's mouths'. At that time, needing to escape from the effeminacy and strained lyricism of late nineteenth century poetry, and from the visions which he discovered he had been imagining outside himself,[16] he had turned to Anglo-Irish dialect because it evoked feeling by naming what directly impinged upon the senses. By 1930, the naming of things within the traditional form of ballad and song provides Yeats with a framework for vision: he is able to combine what Synge had thought were two distinct kinds of poetry, the 'vital' and the 'exalted'.

2 THE BALLADS IN *LAST POEMS*

In the ballads of *Last Poems* Yeats draws upon both Anglo-Scots and Anglo-Irish sources. When he writes about the regular rhyme which he feels is necessary in narrative to achieve 'the fundamental sing-song' of the language, and when he mentions 'ballad cadences' like 'Said lover to the serving maid', ' 'tis sweetly done, 'tis easy done',[17] his terms of reference are taken from the Anglo-Scots ballad. On the other hand, when he says 'What can I do but cry out . . . in simple peasant songs that hide me from the curious?',[18] the model he chooses is from that tradition of the translations from the Gaelic which he also referred to as balladry. One is a tradition in form the other in tone; one is objective, the other rhetorical.

'The Three Bushes' tells the story of the substitution of the chambermaid for the lady in the lover's bed and describes the final union of all three in the common folk-lore motif — which has an Anglo-Irish source in Hyde's *Love Songs of Connacht* — of the rose bushes which intermingle and flower over their graves. The poem is narrative and impersonal, but it contains several syntactical features which are identifiable with Anglo-Irish dialect usage, such as 'that' used as a demonstrative adjective ('That lovely lady said'), or as a relative pronoun (And maybe we are all the same/That strip the body bare'), and 'what' followed by 'but' in order to make an emphatic statement in interrogative form ('Yet what could I but drop down dead/If I lost my chastity?'). The refrain 'O my dear, O my dear' is taken from a song in the 1903 version of Yeats's play *The Hour Glass,* whose source was a translation from the Gaelic by Lady Gregory,[19] which tells of a woman's shameless forsaking of her husband when he gave her the chance to choose between himself or a stranger. Here is Yeats's song:

> I was going the road one day
> (O the brown and the yellow beer),
> And I met with a man that was no right man
> (O my dear, O my dear).

In 'The Three Bushes' Yeats uses this refrain to convey the same sense of regret as in the song from the play, but it becomes much more poignantly wistful by the end of the ballad:

> He bade them take and bury her
> Beside her lady's man,
> And set a rose-tree on her grave,
> And now none living can,
> When they have plucked a rose there,
> Know where its roots began.
> *O my dear, O my dear.*

If the phrasing of 'And now none living can' sounds somewhat unorthodox, if not strained, to the English ear, it is because for the sake of stanzaic rhythm Yeats has compressed his syntax. There is enough precedent in Yeats's poetry for 'And now no living man can'; and the line as it stands in the poem follows the Anglo-Irish mode of concrete specification by retaining the essential adjective which carries with it the sense of the noun it qualifies.

The emphasis of this line links the narrative outline of the ballad with the philosophical theme which is explored in the following sequence of songs: they do not merely tell a story but dramatise the frustration of the conflict between body and soul in the lyrical response of the characters involved. The confident acceptance of 'The Lady's Second Song' is disturbed by its uneasy refrain, *'The Lord have mercy upon us'*, and is belied by the passionate warning of her next song:

> . . . But in honour split his love
> Till either neither have enough,
> That I should hear if we should kiss
> A contrapuntal serpent hiss,
> You, should hand explore a thigh,
> All the labouring heavens sigh.

That the chambermaid merely represents the body is pointed up by the Anglo-Irish connotation of the word 'ranger', which suggests admiration for manhood and virility together with a shadow of alarm:

> How came this ranger
> Now sunk in rest
> Stranger with stranger,
> On my cold breast?

And 'The Chambermaid's Second Song', which was planned originally to be sung after the lover's death, and which concludes the sequence, pertinently qualifies the folk-lore ending of the opening story by reducing the lover's spirit to the same terms as his sexuality:

> From pleasure of the bed,
> Dull as a worm,
> His rod and its butting head
> Limp as a worm,
> His spirit that has fled
> Blind as a worm.

Here, as in 'Crazy Jane Talks with the Bishop', the theme is given concrete reality. The song defines the chambermaid's detachment,[20] and it also exposes the lover as having found an easy way out of the problem posed by the lady and by the whole sequence. Like 'A Last Confession', these songs voice Yeats's contention that the tragedy of sexual intercourse is the perpetual virginity of the soul.

'Colonel Martin' is another narrative and impersonal ballad which is not told merely for the tale's sake. Here Yeats slightly alters a Galway story he had first told in 1910,[21] whose subject, cuckoldry, is part of the stock-in-trade of the street ballad. Apart from the line ' "O what's a wifeless man?" said he', there is no trace of dialect syntax in the poem; its Anglo-Irish and its Yeatsean signature are seen in the fact that it is not so much the events that matter in the story but the attitude of mind, the character they illuminate. In order to intensify the description of the uniqueness of the individual personality, Yeats adds a touch of ruthlessness and cruelty to the character of the Colonel:

> 'And did you keep no gold, Tom?
> You had three kegs', said he.
> 'I never thought of that, Sir.'
> 'Then want before you die.'
> And want he did; for my own grand-dad
> Saw the story's end,
> And Tom made out a living
> From the seaweed on the strand.
> *The Colonel went out sailing.*

Yeats's comment that the ballad has 'a curious pathos which I cannot define'[22] points to a further dimension of meaning: the portrayal of character in action is countered by the muted, perhaps even mocking, tones of the refrain's insistence that life is a vague and lonely voyage.

Such modification or questioning in the refrain of the assertions made in the stanzas is a common feature of

Yeats's last ballads.[23] It is, nevertheless, by their emphasis
on personality that most of these poems are clearly distinguishable from the Anglo-Scots ballad. What interests
Yeats, for example, in 'The O'Rahilly' is the heroic gesture
which defines the man's own sense of himself:

> What remains to sing about
> But of the death he met
> Stretched under a doorway
> Somewhere off Henry Street;
> They that found him found upon
> The door above his head
> 'Here died the O'Rahilly.
> R.I.P.' writ in blood.
> > *How goes the weather?*

Yeats is here of course alluding to the events of the Easter
Rising, but because they are common knowledge he does
not need to specify them.

When Yeats argued in 1906 that 'the minstrel never
dramatised anybody but himself'[24] he had in mind the
Irish, not the Anglo-Scots ballad writer; and in illustration
he quoted a translation from Raftery, the Gaelic peasant
poet. In 1936 he quotes a translation from an earlier native
poet, Egan O'Rahilly, to illustrate essentially the same
feature, which he now calls the creation of personality:[25]

> The periwinkle and the tough dog-fish
> At eventide have got into my dish!
> The great, where are they now! the great had said —
> This is not seemly, bring to him instead
> That which serves his and serves our dignity —
> And that was done.
>
> I am O'Rahilly:
> Here in a distant place I hold my tongue,
> Who once said all his say, when he was young!

Whereas in some of his verse in *The Tower* Yeats's own

self-dramatisation had got out of hand, O'Rahilly's poem
— the opening lines of which Yeats praised as 'a master-
piece of concentrated passion'[26] — avoids what is merely
self-regarding or declamatory both by the concreteness of
its images and by the fact that the personal predicament of
the poet reflects a national catastrophe. As Yeats put it,
'the Gaelic poets of the seventeenth and early eighteenth
centuries wandering, after the flight of the Catholic nobility, among the boorish and ignorant, singing their
loneliness and rage', became a symbol of Irish pride.[27]

In many of the ballads from *Last Poems* Yeats, by
emphasising the personality of the speaker, is working
within the Irish, not the Anglo-Scots tradition. The poems
which have a political figure as their subject do, however,
form a separate group. The two Casement ballads and
Come Gather round me, Parnellites' are closest to the
street ballad tradition, the opening line of the latter being
modelled on a song by the blind nineteenth-century gleeman, Michael Moran ('Zozimus').[28] Yeats was perhaps
underestimating the long memory in Ireland for such
matters when he claimed that his Parnell poem was not
political but 'ancient history. . . . It is a song about a personality far removed from politics of the day'.[29] This cannot be said of the Casement ballads; despite his later
refutation in 'Politics', Yeats in these poems uses a
vigorous public language for what is nothing more than a
public theme. In particular, the rhetoric of 'Roger Casement' is clearly geared to persuade a point of view, and
because that is its sole function this poem is the slightest
of all the late ballads; it is merely a relation of events and
an appeal for redress of wrong:

> Come Tom and Dick, come all the troop
> That cried it far and wide,
> Come from the forger and his desk,
> Desert the perjurer's side;

Come speak your bit in public
That some amends be made
To this most gallant gentleman
That is in quicklime laid.

The rhetoric of 'The Curse of Cromwell', 'The Pilgrim',
'The Wild Old Wicked Man', and 'John Kinsella's Lament
for Mrs. Mary Moore' has a different purpose. The first two
are nearest to the tradition of the laments in the translations from the Gaelic in that each evokes an historical and
topographical memory. But Yeats's theme is different
from that of the Gaelic poets. He is not concerned with a
particular plight in place or time: the personal predicament
exposed in these ballads is used as a framework for metaphor. Their subject is human experience; as Yeats said of
'The Wild Old Wicked Man', they are about 'the history of
the mind'.[30]

A comparison of 'The Curse of Cromwell' with one of
Frank O'Connor's translations from the Gaelic points up
this difference. O'Connor's 'Kilcash' is a translation of a
seventeenth century lament for the woodlands cut down
by the English because they provided shelter for Irish
soldiers after Sarsfield surrendered at Limerick in October
1691. As printed in the Cuala Press *Broadsides* (1937), it
begins:

What shall we do for timber?
    The last of the woods is down.
Kilcash and the house of its glory
    And the bell of the house are gone;
The spot where her lady waited
    That shamed all women for grace
When earls came sailing to greet her
    And Mass was said in that place.

. . . The courtyard's filled with water
    And the great earls where are they?
The earls, the lady, the people
    Beaten into the clay.

Yeats's ballad begins:

> You ask what I have found, and far and wide I go:
> Nothing but Cromwell's house and Cromwell's
>   murderous crew,
> The lovers and the dancers are beaten into the clay,
> And the tall men and the swordsmen and the horsemen,
>   where are they?
> And there is an old beggar wandering in his pride —
> His fathers served their fathers before Christ was crucified.
>
> *O what of that, O what of that,*
> *What is there left to say?*

Yeats helped O'Connor with the wording of some of his translations and, as O'Connor points out, occasionally 'stole' a complete line or phrase for one of his own poems.[31] The first stanza in 'The Curse of Cromwell' combines lines from 'Kilcash' with a line from another O'Connor translation, 'Last Lines', by Egan O'Rahilly: 'My fathers followed theirs before Christ ·was crucified'. Whether or not Yeats first suggested the wording, both his poem and O'Connor's translations pre-suppose a popular audience and evoke their response in the same way. In 'Kilcash' and in Yeats's ballad the speaker immediately involves his listeners by asking rhetorical questions and by naming the things which identify for them their common loss. That the main force of both opening stanzas is not verbal but substantival indicates the poet's assumption that his subject-matter is public: he is confident that to name is to evoke the required response. The rest of 'Kilcash' merely lists what has been lost by the cutting down of the woods. Yeats's poem, however, is not simply about loss and change, but he retains the sense of familiarity with his audience by sticking to the concrete and by using a common idiom which is in part Anglo-Irish in origin: 'what' and 'that' are used rhetorically, the word 'destroys' is used in the dialect sense of 'exhausts', the specific 'clay' is used instead of 'earth', and the unusual idiom '. . . but I

pass their schooling by' is identical with that found in
George Fox's translation. 'The County of Mayo', which
Yeats included in his *Book of Irish Verse* in 1895.[32] The
title of Yeats's poem has of course immediate popular
relevance in Ireland; when P.W.Joyce made his collection
of dialect expressions in 1910, he said that the phrase
meant to put a particularly evil wish on someone.[33]

Whereas O'Connor's 'Kilcash' does not go beyond simple
lament, it is already clear by the second stanza of 'The
Curse of Cromwell' that what is vividly named serves more
than one meaning. Yeats felt it was a very poignant poem
because, he said, 'it was my own state watching romance
and nobility disappear';[34] but the ballad moves out from
the specific identifications of its last stanza into metaphor:

> I came on a great house in the middle of the night,
> Its open lighted doorway and its windows all alight,
> And all my friends were there and made me welcome
>   too;
> But I woke in an old ruin that the winds howled
>   through;
> And when I pay attention I must out and walk
> Among the dogs and horses that understand my talk.
> > *O what of that, O what of that,*
> > *What is there left to say?*

The ruined house is a basic image for the broken power of
the Gael, and it is perfectly fitting that the 'wandering
peasant poet'[35] through whose mouth Yeats speaks in this
poem should talk of the changed order of things as part of
his personal experience; the stanza is also linked to the
tradition of the Gaelic *aisling* or vision poem. But because
Yeats is asserting that 'things both can and cannot be', his
ballad becomes more than lament or *aisling*. Its theme is
the duality of experience: the relationship between the life
of the imagination and everyday reality.

So, too, with the other poems in this major group of the
late ballads: in each case Yeats uses an idiomatic language in

a metre traditionally associated with straightforward narrative in order to illuminate character; and it is the character's self-definition which expresses theme. In 'The Wild Old Wicked Man' and 'John Kinsella's Lament for Mrs. Mary Moore' the speaker, without renouncing an awareness of spiritual reality, openly declares his preference for life. The old man makes his choice to '... forget it all awhile/Upon a woman's breast'; although he has been taught that only God can end suffering, that way out also means the end of existence as he knows it. John Kinsella goes further than this: his Mary Moor '... put a skin/On everything she said' (an Anglo-Irish idiom meaning that she dressed up her tales in her own way);[36] and in comparison with her vitality, Paradise is featureless:

> Who quarrels over halfpennies
>   That plucks the trees for bread?
> *What shall I do for pretty girls*
>   *Now my old bawd is dead?*

The theme of 'The Pilgrim' is much more equivocal. The refrain the speaker sings is a mockery of his penance, which is also a quest, but the poem is nevertheless about that quest:

> All know that all the dead in the world about that
>   place are stuck,
> And that should mother seek her son she'd have but
>   little luck
> Because the fires of Purgatory have ate their shapes
>   away;
> I swear to God I questioned them, and all they had to
>   say
> *Was fol de rol de rolly O.*

A harsher statement than the irony of the last lines of 'Sailing to Byzantium' — which make the point that although man must search for a spiritual reality, he can only understand it in human terms — the refrain in 'The Pilgrim' affirms that nonsense is the only answer which can be given to questions about a different kind of existence. And, whether he is drunk or out of his wits again, or merely deluding into thinking that his words have meaning, the Pilgrim does return from his encounter with the holy man, with the dead, and with the spirit of evil represented by the 'great black ragged bird', to the public house which is his familiar world. Vision, even if it is a mockery, can only be stated in terms of common experience; embodied, not known.[37]

These ballads employ a full battery of rhetorical means to draw the listener's attention, but not at all to the rhetorical end of persuasion. Like the translations from the Gaelic which lament the fall of chieftains or portray the predicament of the professional poet who has lost his patron, their purpose is not to incite or persuade but to reveal the personality, the passion of the individual. The difference is that in Yeats's ballads the predicament is the human condition; and the theme, supplementing that of *Last Poems* as a whole, is the heroic praise of 'the foul rag-and-bone shop of the heart', a frank public confession of commitment to life.

Although Yeats insisted that he must 'write for the ear' in order to be 'instantly understood as when actor or folk singer stands before an audience',[38] he never became popular. Perhaps to be genuinely so, the poet, like Burns (or indeed in a very different and much more limited way, like the Young Irelanders), needs to reflect the habits of mind of a whole community; or like the eighteenth century Gaelic poet, express his feelings in the context of national events. Nevertheless, what Yeats learned from his native heritage in ballad and song gives a recognisable accent to his universality as a poet. To transpose one of his own statements: the shape of a style is from the seed.[39]

Notes

Abbreviations:

Au   *Autobiographies* (New York: Macmillan, 1938; London: Macmillan, 1955).

B of IV *A Book of Irish Verse* (London: Methuen, 1895; revised ed. 1900).

E & I   *Essays and Introductions* (London: Macmillan; New York: Macmillan, 1961).

Exp   *Explorations* (London: Macmillan, 1962; New York: Macmillan, 1963).

LDW   *Letters on Poetry from W. B. Yeats to Dorothy Wellesley,* ed. Dorothy Wellesley (London: O.U.P., 1964).

Letters *The Letters of W. B. Yeats,* ed. Allan Wade (London: Hart-Davis, 1954).

LKT   *W. B. Yeats: Letters to Katharine Tynan,* ed. Roger McHugh (Dublin: Clonmore & Reynolds; New York: McMullen, 1953).

LNI   *Letters to the New Island,* ed. with an introduction by Horace Reynolds, preface by W. B. Yeats (Cambridge, Mass.: Harvard University Press, 1934).

Myth *Mythologies* (London: Macmillan; New York: Macmillan, 1959).

Var   *The Variorum Edition of the Poems of W. B. Yeats,* ed. Peter Allt and Russell K. Alspach (New York: Macmillan, 1957; London: Macmillan, 1961).

CHAPTER 1

1 *Au,* 101.
2 *Letters,* 213.
3 'The Poetry of Sir Samuel Ferguson', *The Irish Fireside* (9 Oct 1886).
4 *Au,* 96.
5 *E & I,* 256.
6 *Au,* 102.
7 *LNI,* 155.
8 Ibid., 172.
9 Ibid., 167-8. See also Yeats's article, 'A Poet We Have Neglected', *United Ireland* (12 Dec 1891).

10 *LKT*, 132.
11 *Au*, 471.
12 *Exp*, 233.
13 Ibid., 156-7.
14 'Popular Ballad Poetry of Ireland', *Leisure Hour* (Nov 1889) 37.
15 'The Poetry of Sir Samuel Ferguson', *Dublin University Review*, vol. II, no. 11 (Nov 1886) 938.
16 *LNI*, 175-6.
17 Ibid., 190.
18 'Miss Tynan's New Book', *The Irish Fireside* (9 July 1887).
19 *Myth*, 1.
20 *Letters*, 66.
21 *Var*, 844, 854.
22 'Young Ireland', *The Bookman* (Jan 1897) 120.
23 *Au*, 188.
24 'The Ballad of Father O'Hart' from a history of certain parishes, "The Ballad of Moll Magee' from a sermon given at Howth, 'The Ballad of the Foxhunter' from C. J. Kickham's novel *Knocknagow* (1879), 'The Ballad of Father Gilligan' from the Kerry version of an old folk-tale.
25 *LKT*, 61.
26 Ibid., 49-50.
27 Compare Yeats's statements in *E & I*, 5 with those in *Au*, 74 and 372.
28 *Letters*, 161, 204.
29 *Au*, 153.
30 P. J. McCall, *Ballad Collection MSS*, National Library, Dublin, vol. 6, p. 3. (I am indebted to Michael Yeats for this reference.)
31 *LKT*, 66.
32 Thomas Parkinson, *W. B. Yeats: Self-Critic* (Berkeley and Los Angeles, 1951), 1973.
33 *Myth*, 13.
34 *Exp*, 220.
35 *Letters*, 148; *Var*, 797.
36 'Popular Ballad Poetry of Ireland', 34.

CHAPTER II

1 'Poems by Miss Tynan', *The Evening Herald* [Dublin] (2 Jan 1892). (This review is not listed in J. P. Frayne's *Uncollected Prose by W. B. Yeats. First Reviews and Articles: 1886-1896.* (London and New York, 1970)).
2 Introduction to the poetry of Ellen O'Leary by W. B. Yeats in *The Poets and Poetry of the Century: Joanna Baillie to Mathilde Blind*, ed. Alfred H. Miles (London, 1892) 449-52.
3 *United Ireland* (27 May 1893). Yeats's lecture is reported verbatim from the meeting of the National Literary Society in Molesworth Hall, Dublin, 19 May 1893.

4 *E & I*, 248-9.
5 'Modern Ireland: An Address given to American Audiences between 1932-33', *Irish Renaissance*, ed. Robin Skelton and David R. Clark (Dublin, 1965) 16, 19.
6 *Exp*, 343, 372.
7 See the following articles by Yeats: 'Irish National Literature 1: From Callanan to Carleton', *The Bookman* (July 1895) 105-7; 'The New Irish Library', ibid. (June 1896) 93-4; 'Young Ireland', ibid. (Jan 1897) 120. (After 1900 there are numerous references in Yeats's published prose to the narrowness of the Young Ireland ideal.)
8 *Letters*, 286.
9 *B of IV* (1900) preface, xiii-xiv.
10 *Lady Gregory Papers* (Berg Collection, New York Public Library) T.S. acc. no. 65B 3563, n.d. (*c.* 1899).
11 *Exp*, 401.
12 *The Secret Rose* (London, 1897) vii.
13 *E & I*, 206.
14 *Letters*, 307; 'The Literary Movement in Ireland', *Ideals in Ireland*, ed. Lady Gregory (London, 1901) 101.
15 *E & I*, 193.
16 'Mr. Rhys' Welsh Ballads', *The Bookman* (April 1898) 14-15.
17 *LKT*, 143-4.
18 *Letters*, 239.
19 *B of IV* (1895) xxii.
20 *Letters*, 205.
21 *B of IV* (1895) xii.
22 'Irish National Literature 1', 105.
23 See Thomas MacDonagh, *Literature in Ireland* (London, 1918) 8, 53, 55, and 59; Padraic Colum (ed.), *The Poems of Sir Samuel Ferguson* (Dublin and New York, 1963) introduction; Robert O'Driscoll, 'Two Voices: One Beginning', *University Review* [Dublin] vol. III, no. 8 (1965) 89.
24 'Irish National Literature 1', 106.
25 'Irish National Literature 111: Contemporary Irish Poets', *The Bookman* (Sep 1895) 169.
26 *E & I*, 180-1.
27 *Letters*, 343, 434-5; *E & I*, 415.
28 *E & I*, 8.
29 'The Literary Movement in Ireland', 94.
30 *E & I*, 266.
31 *Var*, 851.
32 'Anglo-Irish Ballads', *Broadsides* (1935).
33 *Var*, 151.
34 Ibid., 806.
35 The Gaelic word '*aisling*' means 'vision' or 'dream'; and the vision the poet sees is the spirit of Ireland as a beautiful woman. For a detailed commentary on this kind of poem see Daniel

Corkery, *The Hidden Ireland* (Dublin, 1925) 126-45; see also Georges-Denis Zimmermann, *Songs of Irish Rebellion* (Dublin, 1967) 88-93; and Patrick C. Power, *The Story of Anglo-Irish Poetry: 1800-1922* (Cork, Washington, 1967) 161.

36 *Exp*, 24-6.
37 *Letters*, 322.
38 *Var*, 803.
39 Richard Ellmann points out that Yeats omitted this stanza because its meaning was implied in the rest of the poem (see *The Identity of Yeats*, 2nd ed. (Faber, 1964) 126). The implication, however, emphasises mood rather than fact.
40 'Young Ireland', *The Bookman* (Jan 1897) 120.
41 *E & I*, 349.
42 Ibid., 208.
43 Robert O'Driscoll argues that a source for the 'Celtic Twilight' movement in Anglo-Irish literature may be seen in some of Sir Samuel Ferguson's original lyrics. (See 'Two Voices: One Beginning', 90). A comparison of Ferguson's 'The Fairy Thorn' with his translations of Gaelic songs shows, however, a marked difference in subject and style.
44 *E & I*, 353-4.
45 *Var*, 803.
46 Ibid., 814.
47 *E & I*, 513.
48 *Var*, 812.
49 *Exp*, 4-5, 29.
50 See Peter Ure, *Yeats the Playwright* (London, New York, 1963) 174-6, for reference to some of the plays in which Lady Gregory is known to have collaborated with Yeats.
51 *E & I*, footnote on page 299.
52 Ibid., 298-9.

CHAPTER III

1 'Popular Ballad Poetry of Ireland', 34.
2 Corkery, *The Hidden Ireland*, 152.
3 'Popular Ballad Poetry of Ireland', 34.
4 'Clarence Mangan', *The Irish Fireside* (12 March 1887).
5 D. J. O'Donoghue (ed.), *The Poems of J. C. Mangan* (Dublin, 1904) xiv.
6 See James Carney, *The Irish Bardic Poet* (Dublin, 1967) for an account of the role of the professional Gaelic poet, with particular reference to Eochaidh O Heoghusa.
7 *B of IV* (1895) xvii.
8 *E & I*, 521-2.
9 David Sutton, *W. B. Yeats and the Irish Ballad Tradition* (unpublished M.A. thesis, 1972; Leicester University Library) 105.
10 *Letters*, 710.

11   *E & I*, 335.
12   *Letters*, 147.
13   *LNI*, 136; see also Yeats's review of Hyde's *Beside the Fire*: 'Irish Folk Tales', *National Observer* (28 Feb 1891), which was reprinted as 'The Four Winds of Desire' in *The Celtic Twilight* (London, 1893). See *Letters*, 88 for Yeats's early praise of Hyde's style.
14   A letter to the editor, *United Ireland* (17 Dec 1892), commenting on the report in that newspaper on 10 December of a lecture by Douglas Hyde on 'The Necessity for De-Anglicising Ireland'.
15   'Irish Language and Irish Literature', letter to the editor, *The Leader* [Dublin] (1 Sept 1900).
16   *E & I*, 271.
17   Ibid., 201.
18   *Letters*, 403.
19   *E & I*, 271.
20   Ibid., 348.
21   Ibid., 266.
22   'Irish National Literature 111'.
23   *Letters*, 353-4; *Exp*, 147 and 166.
24   *Exp*, 94-5.
25   Ibid., 149.
26   George Moore, *Ave* (London, 1911) 56 and 348.
27   *Exp*, 95.
28   Ibid., 93.
29   *Letters*, 583.

CHAPTER IV
 1   *Exp*, 94.
 2   See P. L. Henry, *An Anglo-Irish Dialect of North Roscommon* (Zurich, 1957) 117-19, 123-5, 132-61, 182-204.
 3   Ibid., 120-2 and 198-204.
 4   Ibid., 161-79.
 5   Skelton and Clark (eds), *Irish Renaissance*, 17; see also *Au*, 440.
 6   *The Secret Rose* (1897) 142-3.
 7   Ibid., 157.
 8   *Myth*, 235.
 9   *The Secret Rose* (1897) 167.
10   *Myth*, 241-2.
11   *Lady Gregory Papers*, 'W. B. Yeats: Letters to Lady Gregory; T. L. S. made by Lady Gregory for possible inclusion in her Memoirs', (2 March 1909).
12   *Letters*, 434-5.
13   See Russell K. Alspach (ed.), *The Variorum Edition of the Plays of W. B. Yeats* (New York and London, 1966), 234-5.
14   Ibid.
15   Michael B. Yeats, 'W. B. Yeats and Irish Folk Song', *Southern Folk Lore Quarterly*, XXXI (June 1966) 156. (Michael Yeats

gives a detailed account of his father's sources in Irish folk-song, but does not consider the poetic theory that determined their choice.)

16 See 'Note on the Music' to this play in *The Hour Glass, Cathleen Ni Houlihan, The Pot of Broth* (London, 1904).

17 Douglas Hyde (trans.), *Love Songs of Connacht* (Dublin and London, 1893).

18 Douglas Hyde (trans.), *The Religious Songs of Connacht,* 2 vols (London, 1906) vol. 1, 50.

19 *The Hour Glass, Cathleen Ni Houlihan, The Pot of Broth* (London, 1904) 76-7.

20 Henry, *Anglo-Irish Dialect,* 206.

21 *Poems* (London, 1895) 77.

22 *Letters,* 434-5.

23 See A. Norman Jeffares, *W. B. Yeats: Man & Poet,* 2nd ed. revised (London, 1962) 167.

24 Ezra Pound (trans.), *Certain Noble Plays of Japan: From the Manuscripts of Ernest Fenellosa* (Dundrum, 1916) 1 and 4.

25 Skelton and Clark (eds), *Irish Renaissance,* 17.

26 For a very detailed bibliography on Anglo-Irish dialects see Henry's *An Anglo-Irish Dialect of North Roscommon.* In addition to Henry's text, the references in this chapter are taken from P. W. Joyce, *English As We Speak It In Ireland* (London, Dublin, 1910) which incorporates the findings of Hayden and Hartog's article, 'The Irish Dialect of English', *The Fortnightly Review* (April/May 1909) 775-85, 933-47; and from A. G. Van Hamel, 'On Anglo-Irish Syntax', *Englische Studien, Band* 45 (1912), 272-93.

27 Douglas Hyde (trans.), *Songs Ascribed to Raftery* (Dublin, 1903) 331; see also: *Myth,* 23.

28 Joyce, *English As We Speak It,* 251.

29 Hamel, *On Anglo-Irish Syntax,* 291.

30 Joyce, *English As We Speak It,* 210.

31 Hamel, *On Anglo-Irish Syntax,* 291.

32 MacDonald Emslie, 'Gestures in Scorn of an Audience', *W. B. Yeats: 1865-1965. Centenary Essays,* ed. D. E. S. Maxwell and S. B. Bushrui (Ibadan, 1965) 114-22.

33 Ellmann, *Identity of Yeats,* 138.

34 Henry, *Anglo-Irish Dialect,* 122; see also 99 and 209-10 for Henry's description of the Anglo-Irish usage of 'that' as a relative pronoun.

35 Ellmann, *Identity of Yeats,* 140.

36 Henry, *Anglo-Irish Dialect,* 119.

37 Ibid., 121.

38 Ibid., 122 and 199.

39 Ellmann, *Identity of Yeats,* 135.

40 Henry, *Anglo-Irish Dialect,* 206.

41 Ibid., 117-19.

42 Ibid., 118.
43 Ibid., 195.
44 Ibid., 202.
45 Ibid., 167.
46 *E & I*, 336.

CHAPTER V

1 *Letters*, 477.
2 See Zimmermann, *Songs of Irish Rebellion*, 70-2, 85-6, 255-6.
3 V. C. Clinton-Baddeley, 'Reading Poetry with W. B. Yeats', *London Magazine*, vol. IV, no. 12 (1957) 47.
4 See *Au*, 504.
5 Ibid., 299-300.
6 Ezra Pound, *Make it New* (London, 1934), 244-5.
7 *Var*, 839-40.

CHAPTER VI

1 *Letters*, 716.
2 Ibid., 710.
3 H. J. C. Grierson, 'Lord Byron, Arnold and Swinburne', *The Background of English Literature* (London, 1925) 68-115. Yeats's letter is mainly concerned with this essay, but he does comment on a quotation from Byron given by Grierson in another essay from the same volume: 'Byron and English Society'.
4 See Joseph Hone, *W. B. Yeats: 1865-1939*, 2nd ed. (London, 1962) 296; and Thomas Parkinson, *W. B. Yeats: The Later Poetry* (London, 1964), 184-87.
5 'Irish Poet Honoured', *Irish Times* (15 Nov 1923).
6 *Lady Gregory Papers*, A.L.S. 65B 3256(22 March 1929).
7 *Letters*, 758.
8 *E & I*, 266-7.
9 *Poems and Translations by John Millington Synge,* preface by W. B. Yeats (Dundrum, 1909) vii-viii.
10 *Letters*, 588.
11 See Frank O'Connor's translation of this poem in *Kings, Lords and Commons* (London, 1962) 34-8; see also James Carney, *Early Irish Poetry* (Cork, 1965) 20.
12 *Myth*, 79.
13 *E & I*, 522.
14 *LNI*, preface by W. B. Yeats, xiii.
15 *E & I*, 524.
16 Ibid., 271.
17 *LDW*, 82.
18 *Letters*, 886.
19 See: Roger McHugh, 'James Joyce's Synge-Song,' *Envoy* III, Nov., 1950, 12-16; and Michael B. Yeats, 'W. B. Yeats and Irish Folk Song,' 165-7.

20 *LDW*, 108
21 See Ellmann, *Identity of Yeats*, 205.
22 *Letters*, 896-7.
23 See Ellmann, *Identity of Yeats*, 202-4.
24 *Exp*, 214.
25 W. B. Yeats (ed.), *The Oxford Book of Modern Verse: 1892-1935* (Oxford, 1936) introduction, xiii-xiv.
26 *Au*, 217.
27 *The Oxford Book of Modern Verse* (1936) xiv.
28 Yeats called his Parnell poem 'an old street ballad' (see *LDW*, 126). See *Myth*, 49 for Yeats's quotation of Michael Moran's song in the essay, 'The Last Gleeman'. For a complete version of the song, see *Memoir of Zozimus* (Dublin, 1871) 24.
29 *LDW*, 130.
30 Ibid., 135.
31 O'Connor, *Kings, Lords and Commons*, preface, v.
32 I am indebted to G. S. Fraser for this reference. (See his article, 'Yeats and the Ballad Style', *Shenandoah*, vol. XX1, no. 3, (spring 1970) 177-94.
33 Joyce, *English As We Speak It*, 166.
34 *LDW*, 123.
35 Ibid., 119.
36 See Hyde, *Religious Songs*, vol. 1, 171.
37 *Letters*, 922.
38 *E & I*, 530.
39 *Au*, 441.

Bibliography

I WORKS BY W. B. YEATS

The following lists contain in chronological order only those books, reviews and articles referred to in the text.

(a) Books

The Wanderings of Oisin and Other Poems. London: Kegan Paul, Trench & Co., 1889.

John Sherman and Dhoya. London: Fisher Unwin, 1891 (reprinted 1969, ed. Richard Finneran, Wayne State University Press).

The Celtic Twilight. London: Lawrence and Bullen, 1893.

Poems. London: Fisher Unwin, 1895.

The Secret Rose. London: Lawrence and Bullen, 1897.

The Wind Among the Reeds. London: Elkin Mathews, 1899.

In the Seven Woods. Dundrum: Dun Emer Press, 1903 (reprinted 1971, Cuala Press).

Stories of Red Hanrahan. Dundrum: Dun Emer Press, 1904 (reprinted 1971, Cuala Press).

The Hour Glass, Cathleen Ni Houlihan, The Pot of Broth. London: Bullen, 1904.

The Collected Works in Verse and Prose of William Butler Yeats. 8 vols. Stratford-on-Avon: Bullen, 1908.

Plays in Prose and Verse. London: Macmillan, 1922; New York: Macmillan, 1924.

Early Poems and Stories. London: Macmillan; New York: Macmillan 1925.

Letters to the New Island, ed. with an introduction by Horace Reynolds, preface by W. B. Yeats. Cambridge, Mass.: Harvard University Press, 1934 (reprinted 1970, Harvard U.P.; O.U.P.).

The Collected Poems of W. B. Yeats. London: Macmillan, 1950; New York: Macmillan 1952.

W. B. Yeats: Letters to Katharine Tynan, ed. Roger McHugh. Dublin: Clonmore and Reynolds, 1953.

The Letters of W. B. Yeats, ed. Allan Wade. London: Hart-Davis, 1954.

The Variorum Edition of the Poems of W. B. Yeats, ed. Peter Allt and Russell K. Alspach. New York: Macmillan; London: Macmillan, 1957.

Mythologies. London: Macmillan; New York: Macmillan, 1959.
Autobiographies. New York: Macmillan, 1938; London: Macmillan, 1955.
Explorations. London: Macmillan, 1962; New York: Macmillan, 1963.
The Collected Plays of W. B. Yeats. New York: Macmillan, 1935; London: Macmillan, 1963.
Letters on Poetry from W. B. Yeats to Dorothy Wellesley, ed. Dorothy Wellesley. London: O.U.P., 1964.
The Variorum Edition of the Plays of W. B. Yeats, ed. Russell K. Alspach. London, Melbourne, Toronto: Macmillan; New York: Macmillan 1966.
Uncollected Prose by W. B. Yeats. First Reviews and Articles: 1886-1896, ed. John P. Frayne. London: Macmillan; New York: Columbia University Press, 1970.

(b) Articles, essays, letters to newspapers, reviews
'The Poetry of Sir Samuel Ferguson', *The Irish Fireside,* 9 Oct 1886.
'The Poetry of Sir Samuel Ferguson', *Dublin University Review,* vol. II, no. 11, Nov 1886.
'Clarence Mangan', *The Irish Fireside,* 12 Mar 1887.
'Miss Tynan's New Book', *The Irish Fireside,* 8 July 1887.
'Popular Ballad Poetry of Ireland', *Leisure Hour,* Nov 1889.
'Irish Folk Tales', *National Observer,* 28 Feb 1891.
'A Poet We Have Neglected', *United Ireland,* 12 Dec 1891.
'Poems by Miss Tynan', *Evening Herald* (Dublin) 2 Jan 1892.
Letter to the editor, 'The De-Anglicising of Ireland', *United Ireland,* 17 Dec 1892.
'Ellen O'Leary', *The Poets and Poetry of the Century: Joanna Baillie to Mathilde Blind,* ed. Alfred H. Miles. London: Hutchinson, 1892.
'Nationality and Literature', *United Ireland,* 27 May 1893.
'Irish National Literature 1: From Callanan to Carleton', *The Bookman,* July 1895.
'Irish National Literature 11: Contemporary Prose Writers', *The Bookman,* Aug 1895.
'Irish National Literature 111: Contemporary Irish Poets', *The Bookman,* Sept 1895.
'Irish National Literature 1V: A List of the Best Irish Books', *The Bookman,* Oct 1895.
'The New Irish Library', *The Bookman,* June 1896.
'Young Ireland', *The Bookman,* Jan 1897.
'Mr. Rhys' Welsh Ballads', *The Bookman,* April 1898.
'Irish Language and Irish Literature', letter to the editor, *The Leader* (Dublin) 1 Sept 1900.
'The Literary Movement in Ireland', *Ideals in Ireland,* ed. Lady Gregory. London: The Unicorn, 1901 (reprinted 1972, Lemma).

'Anglo-Irish Ballads', (signed by W. B. Yeats and F. R. Higgins) *Broadsides: A Collection of Old and New Songs.* Dublin: Cuala Press, 1935 (reprinted 1971).

(c) Books edited by Yeats
Fairy and Folk Tales of the Irish Peasantry. London: Walter Scott, 1888.
A Book of Irish Verse. London: Methuen, 1895; 2nd ed. revised, 1900.
Poems and Translations by John Millington Synge. Dundrum: Cuala Press, 1909 (reprinted 1971).
Broadsides: A Collection of Old and New Songs. Dublin: Cuala Press, 1935 (reprinted 1971).
Broadsides: A Collection of New Irish and English Songs. Dublin: Cuala Press, 1937 (reprinted 1971).
The Oxford Book Of Modern Verse: 1892-1935. Oxford: Clarendon Press, 1936 (reprinted 1966).

II UNPUBLISHED MATERIAL
Lady Gregory Papers. Berg Collection, New York Public Library:

Letter from Lady Gregory to Yeats concerning the attacks made on the first performance of *The Countess Cathleen* in 1899. T. S. accession no. 65B 3563, n.d. (*c.* 1899).

Letter from Yeats to Lady Gregory concerning the re-written *Stories of Red Hanrahan.* A typed letter copy made by Lady Gregory for possible inclusion in her Memoirs. 2 March 1909.

Autograph Letter Signed, from Yeats to Lady Gregory. Accession no. 65B 3256. A comment on "momentum", 22 March 1929.

McCall, P. J. *Ballad Collection MSS.* Vol. 6, National Library, Dublin.

III OTHER WORKS
The following lists contain in alphabetical order only those books and articles referred to in the text.

(a) Books
AE [George Russell] (ed.), *New Songs.* Dublin: O'Donoghue, 1904.
Brooke, Charlotte (trans.), *Reliques of Irish Poetry.* Dublin: Bonham, 1789 (reprinted 1970, Schol. Facsimiles).
Carney, James, *Early Irish Poetry.* Cork: Mercier Press, 1965.
    The Irish Bardic Poet. Dublin: Dolmen, 1967.
Colum, Padraic (ed.), *The Poems of Sir Samuel Ferguson.* Dublin: Allen Figgis; Dufour Editions, 1963.
Corkery, Daniel. *The Hidden Ireland.* Dublin: Gill, 1925 (reprinted 1967, Gill and Macmillan).
Duffy, Sir Charles Gavan (ed.), *Ballad Poetry of Ireland.* Dublin: James Duffy, 1845 (reprinted 1973, Schol. Facsimiles).

Ellmann, Richard, *The Identity of Yeats*, 2nd ed. London: Faber and Faber, 1964.

Emslie, MacDonald, 'Gestures in Scorn of an Audience', *W. B. Yeats: 1865-1965. Centenary Essays;* ed. D. E. S. Maxwell and S. B. Bushrui. Ibadan University Press, 1965.

Ferguson, Sir Samuel, *Lays of the Western Gael.* Dublin: Sealy, Bryers and Walker; London: George Bell & Sons, 1865.

Gregory, Lady I. A. (trans.), *Cuchulain of Muirthemne.* London: Murray, 1902 (reprinted 1970, Colin Smythe; O.U.P., New Jersey).

(ed.), *Ideals in Ireland.* London: The Unicorn, 1901 (reprinted 1972, Lemma).

Grierson, H. J. C., *The Background of English Literature.* London: Chatto and Windus, 1925 (reprinted 1960, Chatto and Windus; Barnes and Noble Books).

Hardiman, James (ed.), *Irish Minstrelsy*, 2 vols. London: Robins, 1831 (reprinted 1971, Irish University Press; Barnes and Noble Books).

Henry, P. L., *An Anglo-Irish Dialect of North Roscommon.* Zurich: Aschmann and Scheller, 1957.

Hone, Joseph, *W. B. Yeats: 1865-1939*, 2nd ed. London: Macmillan, 1962.

Hyde, Douglas (trans.), *Beside the Fire.* London: David Nutt, 1890 (reprinted 1973, Irish University Press; Barnes and Noble Books).

(trans.), *Love Songs of Connacht.* London: Fisher Unwin; Dublin: Gill, 1893 (reprinted 1969, Irish University Press; Barnes and Noble Books).

(trans.), *Songs Ascribed to Raftery.* Dublin: Gill, 1903 (reprinted 1973, Irish University Press; Barnes and Noble Books).

(trans.), *The Religious Songs of Connacht*, 2 vols. London: Fisher Unwin, 1906 (reprinted 1972, Irish University Press; Barnes and Noble Books).

Jeffares, A. Norman, *W. B. Yeats: Man and Poet.* 2nd ed. revised. London: Routledge and Kegan Paul, 1962; Barnes and Noble Books, 1966.

Joyce, P. W., *English As We Speak It In Ireland.* London: Longmans Green; Dublin: Gill, 1910 (reprinted 1971: Gale Research Co., Detroit).

MacDonagh, Thomas, *Literature in Ireland.* London: Fisher Unwin, 1918 (reprinted 1970, Kennikat, N.Y.).

Memoir of Zozimus. Dublin: McGlashin and Gill, 1871.

Moore, George. *Ave.* London: Heinemann, 1911.

O'Connor, Frank (trans.), *Kings, Lords and Commons.* London: Macmillan, 1962.

O'Donoghue, D. J. (ed.), *Poems of James Clarence Mangan.* Dublin: Gill, 1904.

Parkinson, Thomas, *W. B. Yeats: Self-Critic.* Berkeley and Los

Angeles: University of California Press, 1951; new ed., 1972.

W. B. Yeats: The Later Poetry. London: Cambridge University Press, 1964; new ed., 1972.

Poems and Ballads of Young Ireland. Dublin: Gill, 1888.

Pound, Ezra (trans.), *Certain Noble Plays of Japan: From the Manuscripts of Ernest Fenellosa.* Dundrum: Cuala Press, 1916 (reprinted 1971).

Make It New. London: Faber, 1934 (reprinted 1971, Scholarly Press).

Power, Patrick C. *The Story of Anglo-Irish Poetry: 1800-1922.* Cork: Mercier Press; Washington: McGrath Publishing Co., 1967.

Skelton, Robin and Clark, David R. (eds), *Irish Renaissance.* Dublin: Dolmen Press, 1965.

Sutton, David. *W. B. Yeats and the Irish Ballad Tradition.* Unpublished M.A. thesis, 1972, Leicester University Library.

The Spirit of the Nation: Ballads and Songs by the Writers of 'The Nation'. Dublin: James Duffy, 1845.

Ure, Peter, *Yeats the Playwright.* London: Routledge and Kegan Paul; New York: Barnes and Noble Books, 1963.

Walsh, Edward (trans.), *Irish Popular Songs.* Dublin: McGlashin, 1847.

(trans.), *Reliques of Irish Jacobite Poetry.* Dublin: John O'Daly, 1844.

Zimmermann, Georges-Denis, *Songs of Irish Rebellion.* Dublin: Allen Figgis, 1967.

(b) Articles and periodicals

Clinton-Baddeley, V.C., 'Reading Poetry with W. B. Yeats', *London Magazine*, vol. IV, no. 12, 1957.

Fraser, George S., 'Yeats and the Ballad Style', *Shenandoah* (Washington and Lee University Review) vol. XXI, no. 3, spring 1970.

Hamel, A. G., 'On Anglo-Irish Syntax', *Englische Studien*, ed. Eugen Koebling. Leipzig: Reisland, 1912.

Hayden, Mary and Hartog, Maurice, 'The Irish Dialect of English', *The Fortnightly Review*, ed. W. L. Courtney, April/May 1909.

'Irish Poet Honoured', *Irish Times*, 15 Nov 1923.

McHugh, Roger, 'James Joyce's Synge-Song', *Envoy*, vol. III, Nov 1950.

O'Driscoll, Robert, 'Two Voices: One Beginning', *University Review* (Dublin) vol. III, no. 8, 1965.

Yeats, Michael B., 'W. B. Yeats and Irish Folk Song', *Southern Folk Lore Quarterly* (University of Florida Press) vol. XXXI, June 1966.

Index